UNDERSTANDING
# AUGUST WILSON

Understanding Contemporary American Literature
Matthew J. Bruccoli, Series Editor

**Volumes on**

Edward Albee • Nicholson Baker • John Barth • Donald Barthelme
The Beats • The Black Mountain Poets • Robert Bly
Raymond Carver • Chicano Literature
Contemporary American Drama
Contemporary American Horror Fiction
Contemporary American Literary Theory
Contemporary American Science Fiction • James Dickey
E. L. Doctorow • John Gardner • George Garrett • John Hawkes
Joseph Heller • John Irving • Randall Jarrell • William Kennedy
Ursula K. Le Guin • Denise Levertov • Bernard Malamud
Carson McCullers • W. S. Merwin • Arthur Miller
Toni Morrison's Fiction • Vladimir Nabokov • Gloria Naylor
Joyce Carol Oates • Tim O'Brien • Flannery O'Connor
Cynthia Ozick • Walker Percy • Katherine Anne Porter
Reynolds Price • Thomas Pynchon • Theodore Roethke • Philip Roth
Hubert Selby, Jr. • Mary Lee Settle • Isaac Bashevis Singer
Jane Smiley • Gary Snyder • William Stafford • Anne Tyler
Kurt Vonnegut • Tennessee Williams • August Wilson

# UNDERSTANDING
# AUGUST
# WILSON

Mary L. Bogumil

University of South Carolina Press

© 1999 University of South Carolina

Published in Columbia, South Carolina, by the
University of South Carolina Press

Manufactured in the United States of America

03   02   01   00          5   4   3   2

**Library of Congress Cataloging-in-Publication Data**

Bogumil, Mary L., 1955
  Understanding August Wilson / Mary L. Bogumil.
    p. cm.   (Understanding contemporary American literature)
  Includes bibliographical references (p. ) and index.


  ISBN 1-57003-252-1
  1. Wilson, August—Criticism and interpretation.   2.   Historical
drama,—American History—and criticism.   3.   Afro-Americans in
literature. I.  Title.  II.  Series.
PS3573.I45677 Z58 1999
812'.54—dc21                                    98-40219

*For Mom, and Dad, and
Michael*

# CONTENTS

# EDITOR'S PREFACE

The volumes of *Understanding Contemporary American Literature* have been planned as guides or companions for students as well as good nonacademic readers. The editor and publisher perceive a need for these volumes because much of the influential contemporary literature makes special demands. Uninitiated readers encounter difficulty in approaching works that depart from the traditional forms and techniques of prose and poetry. Literature relies on conventions, but the conventions keep evolving; new writers form their own conventions—which in time may become familiar. Put simply, *UCAL* provides instruction in how to read certain contemporary writers—identifying and explicating their material, themes, use of language, point of view, structures, symbolism, and responses to experience.

The word *understanding* in the titles was deliberately chosen. Many willing readers lack an adequate understanding of how contemporary literature works; that is, what the author is attempting to express and the means by which it is conveyed. Although the criticism and analysis in the series have been aimed at a level of general accessibility, these introductory volumes are meant to be applied in conjunction with the works they cover. They do not provide a substitute for the works and authors they introduce, but rather prepare the reader for more profitable literary experiences.

M. J. B.

# ACKNOWLEDGMENTS

Writing this book has been a genuine pleasure. My debts are many. Foremost, I am indebted to August Wilson, whose words have enriched my life and the lives of my students. Next, I am indebted to such prominent scholars as Sandra G. Shannon, Kim Pereira, and Alan Nadel, whose close and careful scholarship on Wilson's works has revealed to me that there are always new and refreshing ways to approach an individual text.

On a personal level, I am indebted to Michael Molino, my spouse, for the encouragement and inspiration that he provided; to my mother for her prayers; to my late father, whose potent spirit has guided me along the right path; and finally to the Major family (Hartwell, Ruby, Debbie, and Rodney) and LeKisha Hoover, whose friendship has endured.

# UNDERSTANDING
# AUGUST WILSON

# CHAPTER ONE

# Understanding August Wilson as an African American Playwright

## Life and Overview of Career

On April 27, 1945, August Wilson, the fourth of six children, was born Frederick August Kittel on "The Hill" in Pittsburgh, Pennsylvania. His father was Frederick Kittel, a German baker, and his mother was Daisy Wilson, a cleaning woman. Wilson's white father never lived with the family, and their estrangement persisted throughout Frederick Kittel's life. Years later Wilson's mother married David Bedford, who became Wilson's stepfather. The relationship between Wilson and Bedford was also a conflicted one and became a source for Wilson's drama. Denied the emotional and financial support of his biological father, Wilson embraced the culture of the mother he admired and loved, adopting his mother's maiden name, Wilson, as his own name.

David Bedford is a model for Troy Maxson in *Fences,* and the tense relationship between Wilson and his stepfather is revisited on the stage in the characters Troy and his son Cory. Bedford, a poor but promising high school football star in the 1930s, hoped for a career in medicine but was never offered a scholarship from any Pittsburgh college and eventually turned to crime. While robbing a store, Bedford killed a man; he spent twenty-three years in prison for the crime. After his release, the only job available to Bedford was one in the city's Sewer Department. Like the fictional Troy Maxson in *Fences,* Bedford never realized his athletic aspirations, which he then hoped his stepson would achieve. Wilson failed to meet his stepfather's expectations, though, when he quit his high school football team. Wilson wanted to be a writer, not an athlete.

In 1960 Wilson dropped out of high school after his ninth-grade teacher falsely accused him of plagiarizing a twenty-page paper on Napoleon Bonaparte. Waiting for an apology from his teacher and principal that never came, Wilson hid his decision to leave school from his mother, anticipating her disappointment. Wilson at age sixteen then began working at menial jobs that exposed him to a wide variety of people, some of whom Wilson based his characters on, for example, Sam in *The Janitor* (1985). Assuming the responsibility for his own education, Wilson routinely went to the Pittsburgh Public Library, where he located the "Negro Section" and read the works of such prominent black writers as Ralph Ellison, Langston Hughes, and James Baldwin: "These books were a comfort," Wilson remarked in a 1987 interview. "Just the idea black people would write books. I wanted my book up there, too. I used to dream about being part of the Harlem Renaissance."[1]

Wilson knew he wanted to become a writer. In 1965 he bought his first typewriter and moved into a rooming house, a basement apartment in Pittsburgh's Hill District. Aside from his mother's home, Wilson also drew material for his plays from his immediate environment, a neighborhood whose inhabitants included ex-convicts and drug addicts. He closely listened to their language, speech patterns, and vernacular and studied their personalities. During that time Wilson was making the transition from poet, his initial artistic vocation, to dramatist. From these stories of the street Wilson discovered a larger narrative landscape. That landscape expanded when Wilson first heard the recordings of blues legend Bessie Smith. The blues, in its narrative capacity, had a profound influence on the young Wilson; it was a cultural medium that helped define him and his race. The blues eventually became a recurring motif for Wilson; through it he voiced the African American experience in many of his plays:

> The craft I knew was the craft of poetry and fiction. To my mind, they had to connect and intercept with the craft of playwrighting at some point, and all I had to do was find that point. Fiction was a story told through character and dialogue, and a poem was a distillation of language and images designed to reveal an emotive response to phenomena that brought it into harmony with one's knowledge and experience. Why couldn't a play be both? I thought in order to accomplish that I had to look at black life with an anthropological eye, use language, character, and image to reveal its cultural flashpoints and in the process tell the story that further illuminated them. That is what the blues did.[2]

Learning to become a writer was uppermost in Wilson's mind, and experiences and influences of the late 1960s and early 1970s helped shape his dramatic vision. In 1965 Wilson helped form Pittsburgh's Centre Avenue Poets Theatre Workshop, and three years later, in 1968, along with Rob Penney, Wilson cofounded Pittsburgh's Black Horizon Theatre Company, a volunteer troupe that staged the plays of Amiri Baraka, specifically *Four Black*

*Revolutionary Plays.* Influenced by the Black Power Movement and the Black Arts Movement, Wilson saw Baraka's incendiary works as addressing the experiences and anger of many black Americans. In Baraka, Wilson found a playwright philosophically like himself. Although Wilson acknowledged Baraka's impact upon him as a writer, he nonetheless realized that imitation would not allow him to discover his own voice. But certain early artistic influences played a key role in Wilson's development as a writer: "In terms of influence on my work, I have what I call my four B's: Romare Bearden [the painter]; Imamu Amiri Baraka, the writer; Jorge Luis Borges, the Argentine short-story writer; and the biggest B of all: the blues."[3]

In 1973 Wilson wrote *Recycle,* a play about a troubled marriage that mirrored his marriage to Brenda Burton, a Muslim, that began in 1969 and ended in 1972. In 1970 Wilson and Burton had a daughter, Sakina Ansari. Wilson said his marriage to Burton ultimately failed because he could not in good conscience accept many of the Muslim beliefs. Wilson's 1981 marriage to Judy Oliver, a social worker, also ended in divorce. Today Wilson is married to Constanza Romero, who was the costume designer for *The Piano Lesson.* Throughout this time of successive marriages, Wilson's desire to write plays grew, and he continued to develop his craft with the financial support of such fellowships as the Jerome (1980), Bush (1982), Rockefeller (1984), McKnight (1985), and Guggenheim (1986).

In 1976, after seeing Athol Fugard's *Sizwe Bansi Is Dead,* a play about the South African pass laws—legislation that prohibited blacks without documentation from freely traveling within or out of the country—Wilson was inspired and felt confidence in his own ability to write drama. In plays such as Fugard's and

## UNDERSTANDING AUGUST WILSON

Baraka's, Wilson discovered that playwrights could address political issues in an artistic medium. That year Wilson wrote *The Homecoming,* a play that examines the mystery surrounding its protagonist's death, a character named Blind Willie Johnson based upon blues legend Blind Lemon Jefferson. *The Homecoming* was staged for Kunta Theater, an amateur troupe in Pittsburgh, and was the precursor of Wilson's later play *Ma Rainey's Black Bottom.* Later, in 1977, Wilson was invited by Claude Purdy to Saint Paul, Minnesota, and began to write plays for the director and fellow Pittsburgh native, among them *Black Bart and the Sacred Hills,* a tribute in verse loosely based upon the infamous stagecoach robber Black Bart. In need of money, Wilson also became a scriptwriter for the Science Museum of Minnesota.

Wilson became a recognized playwright through the reception of later plays. *Jitney!* (1979), set in 1971, is a play about a Pittsburgh cab station and its drivers, and *Fullerton Street* (1980), set in the 1940s, deals with a couple whose marriage is doomed as a result of alcoholism and unemployment after the couple relocates from the South to the North. When an early draft of his play *Ma Rainey's Black Bottom* was accepted for production at the O'Neill Workshop in Waterford, Connecticut, in 1982, Wilson's life as an unknown playwright ended. At the O'Neill, Wilson met Lloyd Richards, whose reputation as an actor and foremost as a director impressed Wilson. Richards guided the young playwright and became Wilson's mentor, honing his dramaturgical skills.

In his plays August Wilson gives voice to the disfranchised and marginalized African Americans who have been promised a place and a stake in the American Dream only to find that access to the rights and freedoms promised to all Americans is in fact guarded and exclusive. But the problem is greater than simply portraying African Americans and the predicaments of American life, for Wilson also wants to explore the African roots, the atavistic connection, African Americans have to their ancestors. Wilson simultaneously perpetuates and subverts the tradition of American drama in order to explore the distinct differences between the white American and the African American experiences: "There are and have always been two distinct and parallel traditions in black art: that is, art that is conceived and designed to entertain white society, and the art that feeds the spirit and celebrates the life of black America. . . . The second tradition occurred when the African in the confines of the slave quarters sought to invest his spirit with the strength of his ancestors by conceiving his art, in his song and dance, a world in which he was the spiritual center."[4]

Wilson knows all too well that white society in America has tended to open the door to opportunity, status, and success to a select few minorities who can in turn offer something that society values. And certainly August Wilson is part of this group, having in a very short time garnered much commercial success on Broadway and critical acclaim from literary and theater critics, winning New York Drama Critics Circle Awards, Drama Desk Awards, Tony Awards, and two Pulitzer Prizes. In *Ma Rainey's Black Bottom* (1984), *Fences* (1987), *Joe Turner's Come and Gone* (1988), *The Piano Lesson* (1990), *Two Trains Running* (1992), and *Seven Guitars* (1996) Wilson presents a decade-by-decade portrait of African American life, capturing both the spirit and voice of African Americans. All of these plays, with the exception of *Ma Rainey's Black Bottom,* are set in Pittsburgh.[5]

Wilson has been criticized by some—among them Robert Brustein, longtime drama critic for the *New Republic* and artistic director of the American Repertory Theater—for both his dramatic topics and themes as well as his defiant stance regarding the tradition of *white* American drama: "Presumably Wilson is prepared to cover . . . more theatrical decades of white culpability and black martyrdom. This single-minded documentation of American racism is a worthy if familiar social agenda, and no enlightened person would deny its premise, but as an ongoing artistic program it is monotonous, limited, locked in a perception of victimization."[6] Wilson believes that the American stage has not provided enough room for the voices of his race. He publicly presented his position—what many considered a diatribe—in June 1996 before members of the Theater Communications Group National Conference at Princeton University. In his address titled "The Ground on Which I Stand" Wilson expressed his serious concerns about the American theater's lack of creative and financial support for black artists. According to Wilson, many unknown African American artists are not afforded the opportunity to demonstrate their talent as playwrights, directors, and actors. Unlike Wilson and his dramatic predecessors Ed Bullins and Amiri Baraka, such African American artists have no venue specifically oriented toward the experiences and voices of African Americans. To prove his case, Wilson cited only one theater company, the Crossroads Theater Company in

New Brunswick, New Jersey, which is solely operated by African Americans amid the sixty-six theaters that comprise what is known as the League of Resident Theaters.

If Wilson's strong convictions are redolent of the militant rhetoric of Malcolm X and black nationalism, Robert Brustein, who has taken issue with Wilson's views, says that Wilson himself is the first to admit that the philosophical environment of the 1960s is "the kiln in which I was fired" and that "I am what is known, at least among the followers and supporters of Marcus Garvey, as a 'race man.'"[7] Wilson desires to dispel the myth of racial equality and acculturation on the American stage. As a prominent black playwright, Wilson embraces a defiant stance against the status quo. The status quo in this circumstance is not the white audience that appreciates his plays but those who subsidize and those who select which playwrights and which plays are worthy of recognition.

Lloyd Richards, the director who premiered all of Wilson's plays and the playwright's artistic collaborator and father figure, perceives controversies such as Wilson's polemic against the American theater as pertinent in American theater history: "As a black person growing up and preparing oneself for the theater, with such a paucity of black material to work with and having to utilize the literature of the world to find myself in, with every succeeding generation in which this subject comes up, you get a little tired of going around that circle. . . . But the good thing is that each time we go around it, for each generation, some progress is made."[8] Although Richards was commenting upon color-blind casting, black actors playing traditionally white roles—all of which Wilson disdains—the remark regarding the paucity of black material stresses Wilson's point that more black theater is needed. Since there are not enough works by black playwrights for black actors to perform and not enough stages on which to perform these works, the African American voice is rarely heard.

Wilson does not accept, in Richards's words, "minuscule progress"; rather, his convictions demand revolutionary rhetoric and zeal to effect a change on the American stage: "Largely through my plays, what the theaters have found out is that they had this white audience that was starving to get a little understanding of what was happening to the black population, because they very seldom come into contact with them, so they're curious."[9] Wilson's strategy of writing a play for each decade of the twentieth century focuses attention on this long journey with little progress and change, one that so many African Americans have taken. Wilson is thus skeptical about assertions of progress and sensitive toward existing definitions and assumptions about African Americans. And ultimately Wilson is committed to a drama that explores and exposes the past: "Blacks in America want to forget about slavery—the stigma, the shame. That's the wrong move. If you can't be who you are, who can you be? How can you know what to do? We have our history. We have our book, which is the blues. And we forget it all."[10]

Skeptical of the tradition handed down to him in American drama by white dramatists, Wilson harkens to the African oral tradition in his plays. This oral history, as dramatized in Wilson's plays, involves a wide variety of stories of spiritual reconciliation. These stories diverge from an historical account in an objective sense in order to incorporate this mystical dimension as expressions of personal will. The characters' stories become a means of self-authentication in which each character draws upon broader, African cultural identity for spiritual solace. For example, in *Fences,* when Troy Maxson tells Jim Bono the "story" of the furniture he purchased, Troy adds his own variation on the topic, embellishing events to suit his own will and desires, and it is up to his wife Rose to intrude with the facts of the case. The oral tradition that Wilson elevates often creates identity rather than records history in any "factual" sense. The stories Wilson's characters convey create an environment in which they can locate themselves and convey their experiences, even when the dominant social, economic, and political environment offers little or no room for them.

Wilson's use of the African oral tradition comes from his insistence on a distinctive African American drama, necessary because, the playwright holds, white society does not share certain important, even unique, qualities that African Americans do share. As Michael Awkward remarks, Wilson's points about race "demonstrate the continuing impact of a belief that the cultural manifestations of 'race' or its performative dimensions remain ideally the province—the possession, if you will—of the group who has produced them."[11] But Wilson seems by implication to take this belief a step further when his characters employ an oral tradition for existential purposes. For example, Troy in part builds up his own identity and his own philosophy of life through the stories he relates to Bono, who in turn finds them valuable and influential. What really happened does not matter so much as the self-definition, confidence, and connection these characters experience from the act of telling their stories.

# UNDERSTANDING AUGUST WILSON

Despite his skepticism regarding the dominant tradition in American drama, Wilson has undoubtedly borrowed from or tapped into the tradition of realistic drama at times while retaining the freedom to deviate from it at others. Such decisions to amend tradition do not simply represent Wilson's attempt to "make it new," to use Ezra Pound's phrase, but to question the assumptions that the tradition is founded upon. Harry J. Elam, Jr., discussing *Fences,* argues that the "unexpected, non-realistic conclusion to [Wilson's] plays suggests that realism itself is problematic and inadequate to accommodate certain cultural experiences or expressions of the current postmodern condition."[12] Therefore, if Wilson can be traced back to the tradition of American drama that led to Tennessee Williams, Arthur Miller, and Eugene O'Neill, he can also be distinguished from that tradition despite his variations upon its techniques and his skepticism toward its tenets.

One of the techniques Wilson deftly employs is what Charles Lyons calls a "retrospective structure," in which the audience learns about the life and experiences of the characters during the seemingly linear development of the play.[13] In order to examine a present in which African American characters struggle within the socio-economic climate of the twentieth century, Wilson revisits the past. Wilson believes that "you should start making connections to your parents and to your grandparents and [start] working backwards."[14] Through the retrospective structure Wilson dramatizes the forces and factors that influence or determine a character's actions in the present—thereby exploring a prevalent theme in modern literature, the impact of the past upon the present. Moreover, this form of developmental structure allows Wilson to express the various influences on a character, including those that are distinctively American and those that are distinctively African. How and where these two decidedly different influences occur in the play often reveal Wilson's attempt to disrupt the traditional realistic development of American drama and present in his plays an atavistic element that links the African American to his or her African heritage.

For example, in *Ma Rainey's Black Bottom,* set in a 1920s recording studio, Wilson reexamines the cultural repercussions of the past in blues musician Toledo's reference to the black man as a "left over" from white American history. Through allusions to the institution of slavery and America's industrial age, Toledo perceives the black man as no longer of use to the whites. In *Fences,* set in the 1950s, Troy Maxson's conflict with his son Cory over Cory's football scholarship echoes Troy's inner conflict with his own sharecropper father. Troy, a garbage collector, tries to negate the legacy of Cory's ancestors in his recollection of a bestial, broken sharecropper surviving during the Reconstruction Era. Set in a 1911 boardinghouse, *Joe Turner's Come and Gone* focuses upon the atavistic ghost within Herald Loomis. This ghost is Loomis's legacy as a post–Emancipation Proclamation black. In the play Loomis's personal experience with peonage becomes a horrific legacy connecting him to a long line of African ancestors, from transport on slave ships, the Middle Passage, through enslavement in the antebellum South. It is a sense of imprisonment that still lingers in 1911 in the consciousness of African Americans. In *The Piano Lesson,* set in the Depression Era of the 1930s, Wilson focuses upon a piano as a source of conflict between Berniece and her brother Boy Willie.

## UNDERSTANDING AUGUST WILSON

This piano is their legacy signifying their ancestors' servitude during the time of slavery. Through the apparitions of various spirits—Sutter's ghost, whose ancestor was a white plantation owner named Robert Sutter, and the ghosts of the Yellow Dog train, one of whom is Berniece and Boy Willie's father, Boy Charles, who perished in a boxcar that was set on fire—Wilson presents the continued effects of enslavement to the will of the whites. In *Two Trains Running* Wilson revisits the Great Migration, the exodus of African Americans from the South to the North in search of the promised land, and dramatizes the consequences of this shift in population in the lives of Memphis Lee and the patrons of his restaurant in the late 1960s. Memphis owns and manages a restaurant that soon will become a casualty of the city's renovation plans. During the course of the play several characters discover the importance of perseverance, despite past hardships and injustices that plague their present lives. In his most recent play, *Seven Guitars,* Wilson explores the theme of retribution within the context of 1940s America through old man Hedley's dream of owning a plantation. The plantation becomes Hedley's way to seek retribution for his late father, a black man whom he recalls fondly but nonetheless ashamedly, because Hedley's father was always "under the boot" of the white man.

In an interview with William Plummer, Wilson indicated that he intends to write a play set in 1984, by far the most contemporary setting of his plays to date: "I'm trying to look at what caused the breakdown in the black family to the point where kids started shooting one another."[15] In an interview conducted by Sandra G. Shannon in 1991, Wilson said that he also considered writing a novel and reflected upon the future of African

American literature. Wilson hopes for future African American writers to produce a prolific body of literature. "This is our culture. How can we develop it?"[16] Historically enriched by the African culture, African Americans come from an oral tradition. Historically disadvantaged within the American culture, African Americans were prohibited from learning to read and write. Since African Americans have not been writing long, in contrast to those writers from European cultures, Wilson hopes that African American writers will invest time in the written word and as a result produce works that contribute to the development of the African American culture.

# CHAPTER TWO

# *Ma Rainey's Black Bottom*

In *Ma Rainey's Black Bottom* Wilson carefully conveys a visceral portrait of Chicago in the 1920s—a sense of time, place, and circumstance—through the play's epigraph, a partial lyric from a Blind Lemon Jefferson song; the play's simple setting, a recording studio that houses the band room; and its preface, a confluence of visual images. In doing so, Wilson reveals to the audience that his play involves a complex narrative about the history of the blues, its African American originators, and one of the blues' unique voices, Ma Rainey, born Gertrude Pridgett, who recorded her music from 1923 to 1929.

As the play commences, Wilson sets a divided scene and a divided culture: it is early March 1927 in Chicago, and the urban streets on the Northside are populated by a throng of "millionaires and derelicts, gangsters and roughhouse dandies, whores and Irish grandmothers . . . [a] priest and altar boys . . . [conducting their daily business] and on the city's Southside, [there is a separate throng] of sleepy eyed negroes [who] move lazily toward their cold water flats and rented rooms to await the onslaught of the night."[1] At night these African Americans venture into juke joints—the word *juke* is of West African origin—to sing, play, and experience a music that transforms them into a community. It is a community, within the walls of these juke joints, that sets these people apart from the other ethnic groups, among them the Irish, in the procession of Chicago's socio-economic life that Wilson documents in his preface. These juke joints and the music performed in them offered more than simply a respite from the cultural and economic segregation and oppression that African Americans experienced on a daily basis. These juke joints were the place in which a distinctive form of music known as the blues was heard, a form of music whose roots and spirit represented the unique experiences of African Americans.

According to Francis Davis, author of *The History of the Blues,* despite the etymological origin of the word, *juke* has been reinscribed to elicit a host of other translations in America, including a home for the blues or juke joints: "*Juke* is an African retention, a word meaning 'evil, disorderly, wicked' in Bambara, a language spoken in parts of the Congo. Absorbed into English via Gulla, the language of the blacks in the Georgia Islands, it has since acquired multiple meanings, all redolent of sinful pleasure; to juke is to dance . . . a juke house—frequently doubling as a brothel—was a place to drink, gamble, wreak havoc, and dance to the blues."[2] According to Wilson, the blues is music "that breathes and touches. That connects. That is in itself a way of being, separate and distinct from any other" (xvi). These are words Wilson employs to describe the almost indefinable impact of the blues and its direct relationship to the lives of African Americans. So too, through his play's characters and conflicts, Wilson crafts such a definition to anthropomorphize the blues so that the audience can comprehend its ability to tell the story of African Americans. Moreover, Wilson's play tells the story of the blues' initiators, such as Ma Rainey and the musicians in her band, who survived through their music in the "bruising city" of Chicago (xv).

In an interview with Bill Moyers, Wilson explained why the blues are significant in his plays:

The blues are important primarily because they contain the cultural responses of blacks in America to the situation they find themselves in. Contained in the blues is a philosophical system at work. You get the ideas and the attitudes of a people as part of an oral tradition. This is a way of passing along information. If you're going to tell someone a story, and if you want to keep information alive, you have to make it memorable so that the person hearing it will go tell someone else. This is how it stays alive. The music provides you an emotional reference for the information, and it is sanctioned by the community in the sense that if someone sings the song, other people sing the song. They keep it alive because they sanction the information that it contains.[3]

If a struggle can be inherited, the blues is inherited, for the blues functions as the documentation of those who experience that struggle. It is an inherent tradition in the African American culture. Perhaps another definition of the blues might prove fruitful. Ralph Ellison defined the blues as "an autobiographical chronicle of catastrophe, expressed lyrically."[4] Wilson's play *Ma Rainey's Black Bottom* is in part a biographical account of a blues singer at the peak of her fame as well as Ma Rainey's autobiographical expression of her life experiences. The play is also a portrait of the struggle the blues commemorates.

Those African Americans who between 1915 and 1960 participated in the Great Migration from the South to the industrialized North were seeking what was held out as the promised land. The comparison with the Jewish exodus from Egypt was important because it suggested that struggle and hope are linked with God's promise of a better life in a chosen land. Many southern blacks looked to large northern cities such as Chicago as that place of hope; between 1910 and 1920 the population of Chicago increased from 44,000 to 109,400. Yet for many this supposed promised land was often full of heartache, for finding work to secure a better life was difficult. The story of that promise and heartache was conveyed through the blues.

Historically, the foundation for discrimination against those migrating blacks was established by previous and incoming immigrants from Europe who were also seeking better lives. According to Ronald Takaki in *A Different Mirror,* initially the rage that Irish immigrants felt against their British oppressors was rechanneled toward blacks, often resulting in violent actions against those with whom they had to compete for jobs in the major industrialized cities of the North. When Wilson writes in his preface, "Somewhere the moon has fallen through a window and broken into thirty pieces of silver" (xv), the biblical analogy of betrayal is clear: those African Americans who dared to dream of and hold out faith in the promised land discovered that this promised land did not exist. Irish Americans, though, were not the only people of European heritage who discriminated against African Americans and used their whiteness to subordinate and commercially exploit blacks. In *Ma Rainey's Black Bottom* the characters Mel Sturdyvant and Irvin, the two white men who operate the recording studio, exploit entertainers such as Ma Rainey and the members of her band, even though without the music of these African Americans their capitalistic gains would not exist.

When African Americans went by train to large cities such as Chicago and New York, they took with them music whose lyrics were drawn from their rural folk idiom. One such individual was Ma Rainey, who was born in 1886 on southern soil in Columbus, Georgia. Her parents were black minstrel performers, and she gained popularity as a singer in F. S. Wolcott's Rabbit Foot Minstrels. Later Ma Rainey traveled up North and around the country with her own vaudeville revue, accompanied by her husband William "Pa" Rainey. Recognized as a flamboyant songstress, adorned by her own spectacular creations, jewels and costumes, she paraded onto the stage with her band and situated herself in front of equally magnificent backdrops she also created, such as an enormous cut-out of a gramophone, which gave the appearance of Ma emerging right from the speaker, issuing from and manifesting the music itself. It was not until the 1920s that those patrons of Ma Rainey's music could hear her voice on recordings played on their phonographs. Francis Davis characterizes Ma Rainey's special appeal to her black patrons: "A large part of her appeal to her people was in her material, an assortment of songs drawn from folk sources and originals in the same tradition, unblushing in their treatment of human sexuality and unself-consciously rural in their allusions to fortune tellers, bollweevils, and chain gangs."[5]

It is on the day of Ma Rainey's recording rehearsal that Wilson's play begins. Ma Rainey and her musicians have yet to arrive. Two white men are seen onstage. The manager, Irvin, noted for his ability to control temperamental musicians, enters the band room; nearby Mel Sturdyvant, owner of the recording studio, is seated in the control booth. Wilson describes Sturdyvant as a man who perceives all black musicians as a commodity. Sturdyvant and Irvin have yet to subdue "Madame" Rainey. Despite their pressure, she will not succumb to any of their demands if they infringe upon her integrity as an artist and, most definitely, her integrity as a black woman:

> STURDYVANT: Listen, Irv . . . you keep her in line, okay? I'm holding you responsible for her. . . . If she starts any of her
> . . . . . . . . . . . . . . . . . . . . . . . . . . . . . . . . . . . . .
> IRVIN: Okay, okay, Mel . . . let me handle it.
> STURDYVANT: She's your responsibility. I'm not putting up with any Royal Highness . . . Queen of the Blues bullshit!
> (18)

Ma Rainey, the Mother of the Blues, is rightly the queen of excuses; Ma Rainey does not accommodate. When the recordings do not meet her standards, she *manages* Irvin and Sturdyvant by fabricating excuses, thereby bringing these sessions to a halt.

In act 1 the audience learns that the southern down-home blues style of Ma Rainey is selling well in cities such as Memphis, Birmingham, and Atlanta but not in northern cities. Sturdyvant exclaims to Irvin that "we've got to jazz it up," for "Times are changing" (19). As a result, the number of songs to be recorded by Ma Rainey has been reduced from six to four, including a signature song "Moonshine Blues" made popular by her musical rival Bessie Smith, which suggests that Ma's time as a popular singer is waning and that variations on the old tunes represent the future. Younger musicians like Levee are now proposing to drop "this old jug band shit" (26) in favor of his swing version of "Ma Rainey's Black Bottom," which is a discordant rupture of the tonal harmony typifying traditional blues, for a new, rhythmically sophisticated blues seems to be evolving, revitalizing and competing with the more traditional forms. This time of musical innovation directly corresponds to a movement of political and cultural significance, the Harlem Renaissance. Occurring in the wake of the Great Migration, blacks envisioned change and thrust themselves into the national consciousness through their talent.

During the 1920s a period known as the Harlem Renaissance originated in New York, which became a thriving cultural Mecca where African Americans sought to express their cultural pride and heritage through works of art, music, and literature. In 1923 and in the few years that followed, legendary black artists emerged or, more accurately, gained public recognition: King Oliver, Duke Ellington, Count Basie, and Louis Armstrong. The blues was now revitalized.

In Wilson's play music, specifically the blues, functions as a way both to express the African American cultural experience and to capitalize on the opportunities, limited as they may have been, for financial advancement. Through music, Ma Rainey and her band bring to mind those African Americans whose experiences have been devalued. Just like Berniece in *The Piano Lesson,* who finally plays the piano even though the memories it evokes are filled with pain, Ma knows that singing the blues involves a deeply personal experience, a form of understanding linking the music, the performer, the audience, and the pain of experience. Ma Rainey demonstrates this point when she tells Cutler why whites do not really understand the blues. They cannot fathom how the blues is a natural response to life, for it empowers those who sing and play it with the strength to endure, to transcend the sense of disfranchisement that daily erodes the spirit. "White folks don't understand about the blues. They hear it come out, but they don't know how it got there. They don't understand that's life's way of talking. You don't sing to feel better. You sing 'cause that's a way of understanding life" (82). To understand that sense of disfranchisement and its eroding effects, Wilson focuses on what empowers, what transcends. It is the blues. When Ma Rainey, for instance, encourages her speech-impaired nephew Sylvester to sing, much more is communicated by Wilson than Ma's nurturing abilities. Ma quite literally gives voice to those African Americans who previously had no voice, no venue as she has had through her music to articulate the burden of marginalization. On the surface whites may enjoy listening to the blues, but they will never fully comprehend what lies beneath that surface—a music encoded with a distinctly African, via African American, experience. In the relationships among the band members and between Ma Rainey and her band, the audience is made privy to the potent cultural legacy of the music Ma Rainey and her band created. Unfortunately for these musicians, though, despite the value of their music to their audience, they are open to exploitation by those who own and operate the recording studios and profit from the sales of Ma Rainey's recorded music.

*MA RAINEY'S BLACK BOTTOM*

The band members—Cutler, Slow Drag, Toledo, and Levee—arrive in the studio to record before Ma Rainey does. Much of the first act entails the interaction among the band members, who represent two distinct generations of musicians. It is from these blues musicians that the audience witnesses the forces of musical evolution and capitalism at work. Wilson reveals much about each band member's personality through his musical abilities and attitude toward the music he plays. And while these four band members wait—their main activity throughout much of the play—the audience glimpses the forces at work that eventually turn the band members against one another.

First, Cutler, a guitar player in his mid-fifties, is introduced. He is the band's leader. Cutler's style of playing could be classified as traditional. Cutler plays proficiently. His interpretation of the blues entails playing repetitive chords to support the melodic-centered direction and form of the music.

Second, there is Slow Drag. He is a bass player of similar age whose interpretation of the blues reflects the fundamental rhythmic, harmonic, and melodic nuances found in African music. His style of playing could be characterized as an Americanized derivation of the African.

Third, the audience encounters Toledo, the piano player. He is the only member of the band who can read music. As the only musician "in control of his instrument, he understands and recognizes that its limitations are an extension of himself," but often lacks restraint in disseminating his knowledge of music (20). In *August Wilson and The African American Odyssey,* Kim Pereira clarifies Wilson's description of Toledo's character and style: "To Toledo, style is indistinguishable from content; it is a manifestation in the artist's fidelity to the main musical idea or theme, whatever his improvisations."[6]

Toledo's interpretation of the blues differs from that of the fourth musician in the band, Levee. In the stage directions Wilson reveals much about Levee's style of trumpet playing and his character: "He plays notes wrong frequently. He often gets his skill and talent confused with each other" (23). Within the heart of this musician lies the impulse to experiment, to transform what Levee perceives as old minstrel-like jug-band music, a style he associates with southern black minstrel performers like Ma Rainey. To revitalize the blues, to invest it with a northern urban feel, Levee intends to transform the traditional blues through the act of improvisation. Levee sees this musical transformation as the key to his own economic—perhaps even ontological—transformation. And his success, when it occurs, will provide him with material rewards, like the new shoes he loves so much, and spiritual retribution for the wrongs he and his family have suffered over the years. The blues, then, for Levee represents financial gain and personal revenge.

The central conflict in the play arises over the various interpretations these musicians, including Ma Rainey, give to the blues. Should these musicians maintain the integrity of traditional blues, or should they attempt to reconstruct the blues to reflect the then contemporary spectrum of African American experience as Levee proposes? The conflict is inevitably between those who embrace change and those who resist change. Amiri Baraka in *Blues People* asserts that the change in black music, the blues, corresponded to the sociological change in the African American's external environment: "The one particular referent to the drastic change in the Negro from slavery to 'citizenship' is his music."[7] The music became a way to ennoble oneself, reaffirm one's identity, and, in turn, reinvest in one's cultural community.

Craig Werner astutely identifies the power of African American music like the blues both to articulate the distinct experience of disparate individuals and to create a communal experience that unifies the various individuals. In contrast to T. S. Eliot's concept of an "objective correlative," Werner suggests a subjective correlative at work in such music: "The process requires each individual not to seek a synthesis, to deny the extreme aspects of his/her own experience, but to assert his/her subjectivity in response to other, equally personal and potentially extreme, assertions of experience. Call and response is African American analysis: a process that, by admitting diverse voices and diverse experiences, approximates universality more clearly than any individual analysis."[8] Ma Rainey's success as a blues singer in large part involved her ability to draw her audience into just such an experience—to blend their individual experiences into a collective and compatible experience articulated through and called forth by the blues. Such a connection among performer, music, and audience in large part presumes a simultaneity of experience, the singer performing the music in the presence of and in response to the audience. Ma's forthcoming recorded performance, however, will preclude listeners' direct participation, separating her from her audience.

Ma's presence in the recording studio problematizes the power of her voice and art, which John Tampane identifies as a "gap between an oral time, in which performance was indissolubly linked to the artist's presence, and an aural time, in which performance could be reproduced (or so claimed the supply side) via the technological innovation of recording."[9] Once her voice is recorded, Ma's performance is contained and isolated, made permanent but divorced from the dynamic environment so crucial to the subjective experience of the blues. Ma understands at least part of this conflict when she reveals that her power over Sturdyvant and Irvin ends the moment her voice is imprinted in vinyl: "They don't care about me. All they want is my voice. . . . They ain't got what they wanted yet. As soon as they get my voice down on them recording machines, then it's just like if I'd be some whore and they roll over and put their pants on. Ain't got no use for me then. I know what I'm talking about. You watch" (79). And, of course, the audience does watch, and listen, as Toledo echoes Ma's sentiments with a more chilling metaphor later in the play, "We done sold Africa for the price of tomatoes. We done sold ourselves to the white man in order to be like him" (94).

Toledo, the band member with the greatest concern for his African roots and the keenest insight into the power whites exert over blacks, addresses this point to Levee when he refers to blacks as history's "leftovers," as those left to rediscover their culture, to reclaim their identity after historical disfranchisement in America. Toledo cites the institution of slavery, the forced enslavement of those from diverse tribes of Africa predominately in the southern states, as the basis for a shared history. Through the use of metaphor, Toledo elaborates upon this sense of shared history. Africans were dropped into a pot the way a cook drops the ingredients into "one big" stew. The pot was America, and the stew, through diaspora, was the sociological and anthropological erosion of the black cultural community. With the Emancipation Proclamation came the challenge of reestablishing an African American identity. In Africa, identity involved continuity through one's ancestors, whereas in America identity involves discontinuity because, as Toledo explains, "The colored man is the leftovers" (57). Now the white man had no use for the black man, and the black man became "just a leftover from history" (57). So, as Toledo tells Levee, the challenge now set forth is for the black man to acknowledge the past, even though whites will always think of blacks as "leftovers," but at the same time not lose sight that it is his destiny as a black man to forge his presence in history: "You already got leftovers and you can't do nothing with it. You already making you another history . . ." (56).

Toledo's advice to Levee echoes the tenets of black nationalism, views similar to those expressed by W. E. B. Du Bois. For example, African Americans should invest their energy to develop themselves as a culture if true emancipation is to become a reality in America. For Toledo, emancipation lies in the hands of the African American. To liberate themselves from the historically prescribed nomenclature of "leftovers," African Americans must disregard the white man's traps, which render them an unempowered minority, but they must empower themselves psychologically and politically. Toledo perceives emancipation as a gradual process that strengthens ties to that time and place before the white man's influence.

But such a process is too gradual for an impatient Levee, who wants change now. His means of liberation will be his music. Levee, a southerner by birth, is not motivated by Toledo's rhetoric; rather, he is motivated by retaliation. It seems that only the older Cutler can empathize with the younger musician who vents his rage in his music. In Levee's psyche, the white man must repay a debt because Levee's father was lynched and his mother gang raped by white men. Levee's memories of his widowed mother and the emotional scars "leftover" by her rape are indelible. At age eight Levee tried to defend his mother with his father's knife, but one of the white men seized the knife and left a scar on Levee's chest, marking him with a sign of the white man's power to do as he will over the black man. Consequently, the only vision Levee wishes to foresee is retribution.

The assault on Levee's mother's spirit constitutes his primary motive for revenge. If he can record his music, his interpretation of the blues, Levee feels he can extricate himself from the past. Improvisation signals changing the direction of his life as well as the music. Levee can rise above the white man if he secures a contract from Sturdyvant, thereby establishing himself as a black artist. If Levee must temporarily play the role of acquiescent southern black, with his "Yessirs," feigning an interest in Sturdyvant's musical expertise, which is superficial at best, he will do so. Toledo says of Levee, "He's like all of us . . . spooked up by the white man" (67). In doing so, however, Levee will, in effect, denounce his musical heritage, which the traditional blues represents, to forge his own identity as a prominent black musician, disregarding his predecessors such as Ma Rainey, Cutler, and the older musicians who paved the way for him and whose spirit in part flows through the music he is so quick to alter. He must, to his ultimate misfortune, rely upon the white man to empower him, to open the door to a lucrative and successful musical career. In this way Levee at once marks a change in the traditional blues style occurring in the late 1920s and at the same time relies upon a change in the traditional behavior of white record producers toward black musicians.

Wilson also explores the consequences of change in a series of metaphors that denote change from a uniquely African American perspective. The most relevant among these seems to be Levee's new pair of shoes. Levee purchases a pair of shoes, Florsheims, with the money he has won from Cutler shooting craps and discards his old worn pair, "clodhoppers" like Toledo's (40). This act symbolizes both Levee's break with his southern past and his break with playing the traditional blues, the old jug-band music of southern black minstrels whom his fellow musicians represent. As Levee's says Toledo's shoes are not suitable for dancing to the modern blues. Levee also notices physical changes in the band room, focusing his attention upon a door he says was not there before. This door symbolizes the means of escape Levee hopes a recording contract with Sturdyvant will afford him. But this door also foreshadows Sturdyvant's rejection of Levee's new arrangement of Ma Rainey's blues—a door to opportunity closed in Levee's face. Levee and Toledo argue over this door, and the events that end the play are adumbrated in this exchange:

> TOLEDO: What the hell you think I was saying? Things change. The air and everything. Now you gonna say you was saying it. You gonna fit two propositions on the same track . . . run them into each other, and because they crash, you gonna say it's the same train.

LEVEE: Now this nigger talking about trains! We done went from the air to the skin to the door . . . and now trains. (25)

The image of the train at once represents a journey toward change on many levels: from the journey made by African Americans during the Great Migration north to the gradual confluence of new forms of black music, which Levee embraces over Ma Rainey's traditional blues. But Toledo and Levee are also two trains on the same track heading right for each other, as their violent exchange ending the play reveals.

In many of Wilson's plays moments of historical change cause moments of personal crisis. Historical change is often problematic and difficult for characters to understand when it is occurring, often resulting in destructive acts. It is the younger generation, represented by the character of Levee, that fails to comprehend fully the implications of change and negates the wisdom and heritage the older generation has to offer.

Cutler's story about the Reverend Gates illustrates quite clearly that the journey toward change is often curtailed by prejudice. His story also reveals the inherent dangers of imitating the white man and assuming a common ground uniting blacks and whites. The Reverend Gates adopts the white man's religion, Christianity, imitating the white man only to be tormented by him, or, as Toledo exclaims to Levee, selling himself to the white man in an effort to be like him. Toledo forewarns that such efforts at imitating the white man will be regretted. Toledo knows this firsthand, for his wife left him when she became a good Christian woman and discovered he could not "do right by her god" (91).

## *MA RAINEY'S BLACK BOTTOM*

Like Toledo, Ma Rainey cannot affect imitation. She realizes the only way to survive in the white man's world is through her music. When she arrives with her nephew Sylvester and her lover Dussie Mae, Ma allows them to assert themselves in a profession in which black patrons have built her reputation while whites have capitalized on that very same reputation and exploited her as if she were a whore. It is Madame Rainey who demonstrates to them that white record producers like Sturdyvant and white managers like Irvin need her. This need is validated by her recording contract and by Irvin's bribe to the white police officer who attempted to charge her with assault and battery after a white cab driver refused to drive "colored folks" to their destination.

Ma Rainey, among all the female characters in Wilson's plays, seems to be the only black woman who dares to defy the hegemony of males, be they white or black. Ma promptly fires Levee when she hears his version of her signature song, and she refuses to sign the contract for the record's release until Sturdyvant agrees to pay Sylvester. Obviously Ma Rainey knows how to bargain in the white man's world. Ma comes to the studio with her name and reputation already established from years of singing and entertaining on the road, unlike Levee who looks for fame and fortune within his surroundings. What Levee fails to appreciate is that Ma's powers of negotiation spring from the guarantee Sturdyvant and Irvin have that her music will sell. That guarantee comes from both Ma's understanding of the innate power of the blues and her long history of singing to southern blacks in their own environment about their own experiences. And it is only that guarantee of commercial success that empowers Ma in the studio. As Eileen Crawford points out, "This is at the heart of Ma's conflict with Levee. The values that inform her artistic integrity are the same that make her the troubadour-as-artist—her loyalty to friends and family and her independence from those that would subvert her art."[10]

For Slow Drag, Cutler, and Toledo the reward for their artistic efforts comes in the form of cash. The three hope to receive their wages in cash rather than in the form of a check. As Cutler states, the black man has a difficult time cashing a check because the white man assumes he has stolen it. Levee, conversely, thinks he can negotiate in the white man's world and that Sturdyvant will offer him a recording contract and money comparable to Ma's for his songs. Sturdyvant does offer him a paltry five dollars for his songs but no recording contract, and he inadvertently slams the door in Levee's face. Once the door to negotiation in the music industry is closed to him and Toledo steps on one of his new shoes, Levee can no longer tolerate those he feels conspire against him, whether white or black. Levee stabs the older musician in the back. Thus, through this violent act he refuses to be a "leftover" and retaliates against those who marginalize his talent and dignity.

As James C. McKelly explains, Levee is trapped in Sturdyvant's hierarchically structured environment, the northern recording studio in which black musicians receive their orders from a white manager and studio owner through a horn:

Wilson's set . . . provides a physical structure that is the symbolic embodiment of these hierarchies which nascent African-American artistic production must fight for birth. The lowest rung in the studio ladder, in the basement of

> the building, is the band room, where the players can re-
> lax between sessions. . . . The studio itself, on a level above
> the band room, is Ma's turf, where the material and ar-
> rangements played by the band must suit her, and where
> she demands the respect of the producer, if she is to per-
> form. Above the studio, accessible by a spiral staircase, is
> the control room, in which the technology of the record-
> ing process is kept and manipulated, without which the
> session cannot be reproduced.[11]

Thus, Levee cannot tap into the source of the power that gives
Ma her strength as a singer and her influence over Sturdyvant
and Irvin, nor can he pass through the door leading to success
and fame because Sturdyvant slams that door in his face. Ironically, he remains "a muted trumpet [forever] struggling for the
highest of possibilities and blowing pain and warning" (111).

However, Ma is in part at fault in that she fails to provide
Levee with the opportunity to develop his own style of music, to
create and perform his own song. While Ma protects and extols
the subservient Sylvester and Dussie Mae, she fails to understand and take charge of this moment in order to advance herself
or Levee. Though Ma may not see the need for change in herself, she too thwarts any hope Levee may have for advancement, misguided as his trust and hopes may be, and the tragic
results are violence against one black man and undoubtedly the
downfall of another.

# CHAPTER THREE

# *Fences*

In *Fences* a fence is much more than the structural partition fifty-three-year-old Troy Maxson builds around his somewhat dilapidated two-story brick home in Pittsburgh; it is a psychological manifestation of his spirit for survival. A fence, therefore, becomes the central metaphor in the play. As Troy's friend Jim Bono claims, "Some people build fences to keep people out . . . and other people build fences to keep people in. . . ."[1] In the course of the play, Troy Maxson builds fences in order to exert control over all those whom he encounters, including himself: fences between himself and his wife through his infidelity with Alberta; between himself and his son Cory through his denial of a father's affection and refusal to sign Cory's football scholarship recruitment papers; between himself and his brother Gabriel (Gabe) through his signature on commitment papers he cannot read; between himself and his best friend in the workplace, Jim Bono, when he secures a job as a garbage truck driver instead of a collector; and within himself when he drinks to dispel those demons of birthright, age, and, most important, discrimination.

If a character is measured by strengths and weaknesses, then Troy Maxson is an imposing figure in both cases. Sources of strength and weakness comprise Troy Maxson; he struggles as a son, as a husband, as a lover, as a father, as a friend, and as a black man in 1950s America. Troy's obstacles are numerous and their psychological impact exacting upon him: an absent mother or mother figure, an unloving and quick-tempered sharecropper father, an unfulfilled career as a baseball player, a life of crime followed by a stint in the penitentiary. In addition his promiscuity has led to the birth of his first son, Lyons, and then the birth of his illegitimate daughter, Raynell. Troy also has been the custodial guardian of his wounded, mentally impaired brother Gabe, a veteran of World War II now with a metal plate in his head and currently a boarder at Miss Pearl's.

Despite his faults, Troy's zest for life, his charisma, his ability to affect the lives of others, all are matched by his capacity to care for others. Although he pays for his home with his brother Gabe's military compensation checks, Troy and Rose take care of Gabe for many years before Gabe decides to become independent and live at Miss Pearl's boardinghouse. Troy is responsible for the well-being of Gabe, housing him, taking care of his money, paying his way out of jail for disturbing the peace, and signing the papers for his hospitalization. Troy confesses to Rose the guilt he feels over taking Gabe's money to improve and pay for his home: "Man go over there and fight the war . . . and they give him a lousy three thousand dollars. And I had to swoop down on that" (28).

Troy also attempts to spare his son Cory the discrimination on the football playing field and from those in the world who do not value the African American. From dialogue between Rose and Troy, the audience can also comprehend his attentiveness as her lover. In fact, the love he shows Rose almost ensures that she overlook his faults. Even after his lover, Alberta, dies, Troy senses his paternal responsibility for their daughter Raynell, whom he brings home and convinces Rose to raise. Troy loans money to his son Lyons, who only drops by when he needs money, never actually expecting repayment, despite his reservations about Lyons's halting career as a local musician and his unstable marriage to Bonnie. With Bono, Troy shares his whiskey, his satirical humor—for example, when he bets Bono that he will complete the fence before Bono buys his wife Lucille a refrigerator—and his convictions about life from his back-porch pulpit. Troy is a confidante to Bono on such matters as work, Bono's wife Lucille, and a black man's spirit for survival in a white world. And it is through all these traits collectively that Wilson creates the larger-than-life and complex character of Troy Maxson.

Troy subverts the stereotypical view of the African American male—the lazy, shiftless, inarticulate, and irresponsible man who abandons his family. Wilson has expressed a desire to countermand the prevailing image of black men: "'I know there are not strong black images in literature and film, so I thought, why not create them? . . . Troy Maxson is responsible. Those images are important. Every black man did not just make a baby and run off.'"[2] Troy articulates admirably the ideal of masculine loyalty and duty to family. He holds his responsibility as breadwinner central to his identity, a view held by many men of his generation, regardless of ethnicity.

In the opening scene of *Fences,* when Troy and Bono discuss an encounter between a black man and a white man, Wilson dispels the long-standing traditional representation of African American males perpetuated in American drama. Michael Awkward sees this scene between Troy and Bono as fundamental to Wilson's overall dramatic plan: "the play's opening scene attempts to bracket or set containing boundaries around traditional notions of black theatrical representation, thereby insisting that what follows will not conform to the nonsense syllables and actions characteristic of black participation in the theater of America historically."[3] Wilson can be seen as placing a fence around his own play in order to dismiss and keep out recurrent notions of black identity that he "ain't got no time for" (2). Thus, the conversation between Troy and Bono announces to the audience that any assumptions they may have made about the identity of these two men should be reassessed. Of course, such efforts cannot entirely negate the long-standing influence of racist stereotypes, but it does present a clear countertext, a mockery of such assumptions. Wilson also takes care, however, to reveal a side of Troy that transcends the particular limitations of his situation. Rather than being completely overwhelmed by life, Troy is in many ways larger than life, a quality that garners him the respect of others. Troy exudes dignity and articulates it in his principles. Through Troy's sense of what is just and his strength of character, this air of dignity permeates Bono's world as well. Troy becomes Bono's role model.

The character of Troy Maxim suggests a particular combination of tradition and innovation. On the one hand, Troy represents an African American male who defies the stereotypes so often thrust upon such characters, both in the past and the present. On the other hand, Troy resembles other memorable male figures in American drama. In this sense *Fences* appears to be a play in the tradition of Eugene O'Neill's *Long Day's Journey into Night* or Arthur Miller's *Death of a Salesman* in which forces external to the family play a key role in the family's internal conflict. Like the importance of the Irish American immigrant experience that so molds James Tyrone's consciousness in O'Neill's play and like the debilitating influence of a materialistic, mechanistic society on Willy Loman's psyche in Miller's play, the lingering and devastating effects of racism and segregation on the conflicted Troy Maxson and his family are portrayed in Wilson's play.

Wilson is careful not to make *Fences* a play that merely rages against injustices the audience will already condemn. Rather, he dramatizes a series of confrontations and revelations among family members that reveal the way racism scars a person's conscience and then is passed on to subsequent generations. While about the family of a black garbage collector in the 1950s, Wilson's play shares traits often found in American drama: a powerful but destructive central character; the house as central location (family as microcosm of society); a concern about professional success, linked with identity, with Troy fixated upon denied opportunity; a conflict with past and present image of self, resulting in a corresponding conflict with children; the need for children to accept or discard parental influence.

But Troy *is* a black man living in America of the 1950s, a time when the Civil Rights Movement was just beginning. Troy and his family live when the seeds of the Civil Rights Movement are about to be sewn, to take root in the 1960s, a time when opportunities for people of color are slowly increasing. Wilson, in his preface to the play, foreshadows this change: "By 1957, . . . the hot winds of change that would make the sixties a turbulent, racing, dangerous, and provocative decade had not yet begun to be blown full."

Troy learned to play baseball in prison, and despite his proficiency at the game, he was barred from making the national

pastime his job because he played before the integration of baseball. Collecting the garbage of whites proves to be the only job
available to him. In the play Troy, who is now too old to play
professional baseball, cannot enter the door opened by Jackie
Robinson. As a result, Troy rages against white racism, Robinson,
and other baseball players who now have the opportunities he
was denied. Troy even denies his son a similar opportunity when
he refuses to sign the permission letter that college football scouts
need to recruit Cory.

Troy, then, represents the lack of professional and personal
opportunities available to African Americans of the time. While
progress had been made when the color barrier was breached,
Troy cannot personally benefit from that progress. His potential
has been lost, existing now only in the oral record of his athletic
prowess that lives on among friends. In fact, Troy can only advance in his current job as a garbage collector by moving from
hauler to driver. So at a time of heady social and racial advances,
Troy merely moves from the back to the front of the garbage
truck—losing his lifelong friendship with Bono in the process.
And therein lie the irrecoverable loss, pain, and alienation of
Troy Maxim.

Some of the negative views Troy espouses are of course
anachronisms, for he tends to dwell on the past. When Troy insists that there are no black sports figures in baseball, Rose reminds him of Jackie Robinson. In fact, Troy often reminds both
Rose and Cory that there will never be anyone to surpass him in
skill. If it were not for the lack of opportunity and now his age,
Troy believes that he would have been the best baseball player

ever to play the game. Therefore, throughout the play the tense relationship between Troy and Cory worsens because Cory lives in a changing America and Troy refuses to detect the change.

Except during his encounter with the union official, which results in a promotion, Troy thinks in terms of the black man's burden in a Jim Crow America, not in terms of an America on the verge of the Civil Rights Movement. This is not to say that Troy's perspective is without historical foundation, but as Rose says, "The world is changing around you and you can't see it" (40). Rose is able to see what Troy cannot when she first mentions Jackie Robinson crossing the color line, a black man who represented the well-deserved and eagerly awaited opportunity for African Americans to excel in a supposedly democratic America. Jackie Robinson's playing field extended further than the baseball diamond; the playing field was America, and the goal was African Americans' right to obtain the American Dream. Nevertheless, Troy Maxson blinds himself to the slow progress for equal rights and constructs a psychological fence against any manifestation of that progress.

Revealing his failure to understand the times he is living in, Troy presciently claims that it is his responsibility to be protective of Cory, to ensure that he does not experience what Troy has as a black man in a white world: "I don't want him to be like me! I want to move as far away from my life as he can get" (39). Troy sincerely conveys his paternal love to Cory the best he can by implying that familial kinship, often a great burden, is one he prizes in his role as a father. When Cory complains to Rose on the day of Troy's funeral that he lives in Troy's shadow, that "I want to be me," Rose replies that Cory cannot deny the influence that Troy had over his life, nor deny that he too possesses his father's tenacious spirit to survive: "That shadow wasn't nothing but you growing into yourself" (97). Until Cory consciously realizes the inevitable fact that his identity emerges from his father's, he is unable to forgive Troy for his shortcomings. Rose's words to her son ring true and are testimonial to Troy as a caring, but flawed, father to Cory. The epigraph to the play imparts the same truth Cory must discover at the play's end: "When the sins of our fathers visit us / We do not have to play host. / We can banish them with forgiveness / As God, in His Largeness and Laws." At the play's end Cory Maxson, now a corporal in the marines on a path he has chosen, learns that he continues that legacy. His father was a survivor in his tenacity to remain proud in his identity as Troy Maxson—son of a share-cropper who lived in his father's shadow, prospective great base-ball player, and sole preserver of the family.

Wilson thus employs another theme common to American drama—that the sins of the father are visited upon the family, resulting in a financially and psychologically dysfunctional fam-ily that can only cure itself or resolve its conflicts by the purga-tion of the father figure. Such classics of the American stage as *Long Day's Journey into Night* and *Death of a Salesman* are two examples of this basic theme at work. As Charles R. Lyons ar-gues, this "process of exorcising the presence of the father, and assimilating his energy [occurs] by appropriating self-consciously both the aesthetic conventions of realism and the archetypal para-digms in which we perceive the relationships of fathers and sons."[4] While Wilson clearly follows this tradition in part, he also subverts it in part—not only to undercut the stereotype of

African American males but also to deviate from the tradition of non–African American drama and thereby explore a new theme with a new voice.

For instance, Troy is financially responsible, even when he is psychologically destructive. But that destructiveness is a manifestation of Troy's own abusive past and his fervent conviction that life offers no easy options or reliable breaks. At the end of the play there is no exorcism of the father figure or his legacy but rather a communion of the new generation who can now, under the aegis of Gabriel's transcendent song, reconcile themselves with their past and look to the future. The atavistic ritual of Gabriel's song sends Troy on to the next world and unites the family. Harry J. Elam, Jr., describes this event in the play as combining the African Yoruba ritual—which acts as a transition between the worlds of the ancestors, the living, and the unborn— and the Christian soul's flight to heaven: "The 'Christian' Archangel opens the gates of Heaven by engaging in a Yoruban ceremony connecting himself and his family to African traditions. Gabriel invokes a racial memory, an African inheritance. His actions again reinforce the impact of the past on the present as the family's African heritage provides a benediction for their African-American present."[5] Thus, Wilson deftly continues but also subverts both a specific stereotype of African American males and a well-established theme in American drama. And in the process Wilson discovers a distinctive way of exploring the lives of his characters.

The paradox of Troy Maxson is that he stridently advocates self-sacrifice and financial responsibility over expressions of self-fulfillment and self-indulgence while falling prey to the forces of his own contempt. Although Troy is supportive of Lyons throughout the play, he nonetheless casts a suspicious eye on Lyons's musical aspirations, philandering, and laziness. In this way, Troy defines himself and the role of the male in contrast to the behavior demonstrated by this son. However, when Troy justifies his affair with Alberta to Bono, a friend who has in the past looked up to Troy as a role model, even a prophet, his argument sounds more like the words of Lyons Maxson than of Troy Maxson. For in this instance Troy expresses the view that his need for self-fulfillment overrides all other concerns—particularly as long as he fulfills his financial obligations to his family. Perhaps this paradox in Troy's thinking explains his relationship with Lyons.

In contrast to Troy's turbulent relationship with Cory, the relationship between Troy and Lyons is almost amicable. Without trepidation, but nonetheless wary of scrutiny of his desire to be a musician, Lyons, Troy's son from a previous marriage, reminds his father that he is thirty-four years old and that Troy was an absentee father to him. Therefore, Lyons's dream of becoming a successful musician has not been hampered because of the physical and psychological distance between himself and his father. However, that distance has also allowed Lyons to fall prey to a trap Troy knows all too well, that of satisfying one's own desires at the expense of one's responsibilities.

Cory has always lived under Troy's roof whereas Lyons has not. Consequently Lyons never allows Troy to coerce him into taking a "decent" job in rubbish. Troy can talk endlessly to Lyons about economic responsibility to one's family, in Lyons's case his wife Bonnie, but he cannot convince Lyons to change his ways. Lyons is bold in his proclamation that music sustains him: "I just stay with my music cause that's the only way I can live in the world . . ." (18). Unlike Cory, Lyons defines clearly the difference between Troy and himself: "You got your way of dealing with the world . . . I got mine" (18).

Over the years Rose has merely acquiesced to her husband's demands, but Cory has not. When the two are alone together, Cory informs Rose that he will ignore his father's admonition against playing football. As Rose well knows, Cory's dreams of obtaining a college education and playing football matter little if at all to Troy. Troy has reminded Cory that a man's sense of responsibility requires that Cory secure a job to provide food, clothing, and shelter for himself and later his dependents, just as Troy has done. Cory tells Troy that he cannot work for Mr. Stawicki at the A&P and that he will play football because "This way I'll be going to college. I'll get my chance . . ." (36).

In act 2 father and son confront each other, and an enraged Cory expresses his resentment over his father's domination and the loss of his "one chance": "You ain't never gave me nothing but hold me back. Afraid I was gonna be better than you" (87). After Cory has accused Troy of being a poor father, Troy disinherits Cory and tells him that his possessions will be deposited on the other side of the fence. A fence, constructed from Troy Maxson's unyielding conviction to his principles, is erected permanently between father and son. During this crucial opening scene Cory picks up Troy's bat and swings twice at him, missing both times. When Troy advances toward him, Cory is unable to use the bat to strike out against his father. Troy then grabs the bat and stands over a cowering and vanquished Cory, restraining himself from releasing a final blow. At this juncture a stunned Cory leaves. This final assault upon Cory's spirit corresponds to Troy's earlier invocation to Death, replete with baseball metaphor. This connection among Cory, baseball, and Death reveals Troy's inability to see, understand, and accept both that the world is changing and that his time in this world is short.

Death is certainly a complex metaphor within the play and often yoked with baseball: "Death ain't nothing. I done seen him. Done wrassled with him. You can't tell me nothing about death. Death ain't nothing but a fastball on the outside corner" (10). In fact, when Troy describes his severe bout with pneumonia in act 1, the two figuratively merge again: "That's all death is to me. A fastball on the outside corner" (10). Troy constantly wages battle and challenges Death. Troy's life as he sees it has been like a baseball game replete with fastballs, curveballs, sacrifice flies, and numerous strikes against him, and unrelenting Death represents the injustice of the white man. Hence Troy personifies Death along racial lines when he recalls his stay in Mercy Hospital to Bono and Rose: "Death stood up, throwed off his robe . . . had him a white robe with a hood on it . . ." (F12). In Troy's feverish vision, the specter representing the end of his life and impeding his progression into the next life is dressed in the garb of a Ku Klux Klan member. To stave off the personal and social constraints of being a strong-willed black man in a white society, conceived as being in Death's grip, Troy maintains a watchful and vigilant eye. In this battle with Death, including the inevitable Day of Judgment, as his brother Gabriel often reminds everyone, Troy uses "vigilance."

Troy uses what he calls "vigilance" to keep a watch on Death, brandishing the sword of his will to combat God's sword and pierce Death's hold over him:

> I say . . . What do you want, Mr. Death? The Bible say be ever vigilant. That's why I don't get so drunk. I got to keep my watch. (11)
>
> . . . Death ain't nothing to play with . . . as long as I keep my vigilance . . . he's gonna have to fight to get me. I ain't going easy. (12)
>
> Alright . . . Mr. Death. See now . . . I'm going tell you what I'm gonna do. I'm gonna build me a fence around this yard. I ain't gonna fall down on my vigilance this time. (77)

Undeniably this vigilance affects everyone around Troy, for to preserve his pride Troy exerts control over his family through storytelling that presents his version of how things really are.

Bono half-seriously, half-facetiously identifies the tendency in Troy: "I know you got Uncle Remus in your blood. You got more stories than the devil got sinners" (13). Unlike the folktales of Uncle Remus, Troy Maxson's tales do not disguise the hardships that he has endured, and the morals of his stories are always the same—injustice prevails. Even on the day Troy dies, he attempts to fend off Death. Just as Gabriel, believing himself to be the Archangel Gabriel, tries to cast out the imaginary hellhounds he hears at Troy's door, Troy knows that his time is near and that his name is written in St. Peter's book: "I can't taste nothing. Hallelujah! I can't taste nothing no more. (*Troy assumes a batting posture and begins to taunt Death, the fastball in the outside corner.*) Come on! It's between you and me now! I be ready for you . . . but I ain't gonna be easy" (89).

Lloyd Richards, director of Wilson's plays and collaborative muse in their production, asserts in the introduction to the play that for Wilson's powerful character Troy Maxson "Strength of body and of purpose are not enough. Chance and the color of one's skin, chance again, can tip the balance. 'You've got to take the Crooked with the straight'" (viii). While Troy struggles to keep his balance, to be empowered as a black man, he subconsciously constructs and is enclosed by yet another fence, his inability to accept that the times are changing.

Unfortunately, Troy Maxson imparts the worst of himself and the best of himself as he constructs this fence around his family. In his love for Cory, Troy denies Cory his college career and football scholarship, fearing the same limitations that halted his own baseball career. Troy also places more emphasis on financial responsibility than paternal affection, which he sees as preferable to the behavior demonstrated by his father. To Lyons and Bono, Troy explains that a man's responsibility toward his family is something he learned from his restless, philandering father, whose wives had left him to care for eleven kids: "he felt a responsibility toward us . . . but without that responsibility he could have walked off and left us . . . made his own way" (51).

Because of his affair with Alberta, Troy loses the love of his wife as well as the respect of his lifelong friend Bono. When Troy breaks his marriage vows, he becomes much like his older son Lyons—whose preference for pleasure over responsibility, self-fulfillment over familial bonds, had previously distinguished son from father.

But the greatest loss that Troy experiences involves his family relationships and the loss of human compassion and contact that his narrow definition of manhood, father, and husband costs him. By drawing a strict boundary around himself regarding familial relations, Troy loses virtually every sense of affection and bond between himself and his son, causing Cory to conclude that his father does not even like him. Troy may not commit the sin of many African American males, what he terms "the walking blues," but he nonetheless fails to see the need in his son for more than the burden of duty Troy declares as his primary, if not only, obligation to his son: "It's my job. It's my responsibility! You understand that? A man got to take care of his family" (38). In his response to Cory's plea for some kind of parental affection or reaction from his father, Troy reveals that he has thoroughly blended all sense of the personal and the professional, linking the relationship between son and father with the relationship between employer and employed. And just as Troy loses a close relationship with his friend Bono when he advances himself professionally, so too Troy loses any hope of an affectionate relationship with his son by defining their relationship in the language of commerce rather than the language of blood.

Rose dearly desires to preserve the family she has never had: "My whole family is half. . . . Everybody got different fathers and mothers. . ." (68). A fence to Rose has spiritual significance, solace to comfort her during the times she must intervene in the dysfunctional relationship between her son Cory and husband Troy, and on one morning, in the throes of rare domestic bliss, Rose expresses her sense of momentary contentment in song: "Jesus, be a fence all around me every day. / Jesus, I want you to protect me / As I travel on my way" (21). Like a flower waiting to blossom, as a nurturing wife Rose has instilled hope and love in her husband and cultivated the relationship: "I planted a seed and watched and prayed over it. I planted myself inside you and waited to bloom . . ." (71). Rose is shocked and devastated to learn that the man in whom she entrusted her love, her most intimate possession, is unfaithful and therefore not worthy of that love: "Where was 'we' at when you was down there rolling with some god-forsaken woman?" (68). Rose has waited all these years for Troy to realize her significance and to assure her sense of place and destiny only to receive betrayal in its place.

Cory wonders why his mother wants a fence around the yard, and Troy wonders who she is trying to prevent from robbing valuables they do not own or from trespassing on their property. It seems that only Jim Bono knows. Bono explains that Rose wants the fence so she can preserve her sense of a close family and keep everyone together. Rose implicitly shares with Cory her desire and passion for the man who could make this dream possible on the day of Troy's funeral: "I was thirty years old and done seen my share of men. . . . Here is a man that fill all them empty spaces you been tipping around the edges of. One of the empty spaces was being somebody's mother" (97).

Troy is not the only one in the play to experience loss; Rose loses her sense of self in her commitment to her husband. Any hope she has for self-fulfillment is directed toward her family and the husband in whose presence and strength she subsumes her identity: "That was my first mistake. Not to make him leave some room for me" (98). Like Troy, Rose focuses upon the security offered by financial obligation, the house in which she can sing. Rose discovers that financial security is only a portion of the equation and that it can simultaneously take away what it also provides.

Unlike Troy, though, Rose can articulate her failures and convey them to her son in hopes that he will see her and Troy as fallible humans whose mistakes Cory need not duplicate. Rose's self-awareness coupled with her strength of character and capacity for forgiveness ultimately communicates the sense of hope for the future the play presents. While it is Gabriel's song and dance that leads to a sense of spiritual reconciliation between father and children that links the generations, it is Rose's emotional words that convey the power of love that links the generations.

Wilson ingeniously proffers hope in Rose's views, her words providing a sense of renewal and reconciliation. Rose can be seen as the most powerful character in the play because she sees that forgiveness leads to hope rather than despair within the Maxson family. Rose's words to Cory and her willingness to raise Troy's illegitimate daughter, Raynell, articulate coherently the spiritual vision that can only otherwise be expressed through music and dance by the brain-damaged Gabriel. Thus, the play ends with spiritual and personal reconciliation despite all the injustices and pain experienced by the characters. Perhaps the next generation will not suffer the way its predecessor did; perhaps it will not perpetuate the trauma of racism either. In her own way Rose reconciles with Troy the moment she chooses to become surrogate mother to Raynell. So too Cory must reconcile himself with his father on his own terms the day of Troy's funeral.

For the last time Troy wages battle with death, vigilantly swinging his bat only to experience defeat. Whether the cause of Troy's death is a heart attack or simply ill health and age, the physical cause is secondary to the psychological impact of the final scene. In this scene the cumulative effect of Wilson's use of the metaphors of the fence, death, and baseball reveal the complexity of Troy's character, foreshadowing Troy's demise and later a tribute to him the morning of his funeral. In Troy's yard a posthumous tribute expressed by his children Cory and Raynell is the song about their father's dog "old Blue," a song forever inscribed in their memory as one that he sang to them. Soon after, an ecstatic Gabriel enters and blows his worn trumpet, beckoning Saint Peter to open the gates, simultaneously signifying the disintegration of Troy's fences and the willingness of his family to forgive him, both of which usher Troy's soul to heaven.

*Fences* involves a conflict between the characters's desire to break through boundaries, redefine themselves, and discover self-fulfillment and the fences and boundaries erected by society and individuals that limit, hinder, define, or exclude. From the stage directions and setting of the play, the audience knows that certain historical changes are occurring simultaneously with events in the play, and Wilson's play reveals the complexity of those changes and the pain of progress in the lives of a few characters. But *Fences* also offers a sense of hope as Gabriel calls upon Saint Peter to open the gates of heaven and welcome home the ever-vigilant Troy Maxson.

# CHAPTER FOUR

# *Joe Turner's Come and Gone*

The theme of displacement and all its psychological vicissitudes is dramatized in August Wilson's *Joe Turner's Come and Gone,* a play in which the African American residents of a Pittsburgh boardinghouse in 1911 attempt to rediscover, repossess, and redefine themselves historically and socially as free citizens. These children of "newly freed slaves," like others before them, attempt to comprehend and find a place in this polyethnic, and certainly hostile, environment. In order to contrast and magnify the sense of displacement each of these characters of southern origin experiences in the North, Wilson personifies many elements in the setting. The fires of the steel mill rage; the barges trudge up the river; and the city of Pittsburgh flexes it muscles "with a combined sense of industry and progress." Simply put, the environment that Wilson depicts is metaphorically combative. Therefore, the African American characters attempt to build bridges, roads, houses, and tunnels in order to harness or bypass this environment.

In his preface to the play Wilson explains how these African Americans "wander" the city with few personal belongings. With Bibles and guitars in hand, these "marked men and women" attempt to forge new identities as free men and women of substance: "From the deep and near South the sons and daughters of newly freed African slaves wander into the city. Isolated, cut off from memory, having forgotten the names of the gods and only guessing at their faces, they arrive dazed and stunned, their hearts kicking in their chest with a song worth singing . . . marked men and women seeking . . . a new identity as free men of definite and sincere worth . . . they carry as part and parcel of their baggage a long line of separation and dispersement which informs their sensibilities." Like outsiders in a strange land, they attempt to "reconnect" and "reassemble" themselves as free citizens of "definite and sincere worth." Moreover, Wilson asserts that these characters want "to give clear and luminous meaning to [their ethnocentric] song [a voice whether collective or individual] which is [comprised of] both a wail and a whelp of joy." So to understand the meaning of their songs, the audience must situate the experiences and traumas of Wilson's characters within a historical and cultural context in order to appreciate the challenges of each character's attempt to "reconnect" and "reassemble" (often out of conflicting or contradictory influences) his or her identity as an African American living in twentieth-century America.

As a result of the Reconstruction period in the South, and after the 1896 Supreme Court decision in *Plessey v. Ferguson,* the "separate but equal" doctrine, the southern states vehemently began to impose segregation and to enforce Jim Crow laws by rewriting state constitutions and thereby legislating an exclusionist policy toward African Americans. Therefore by 1907 many African Americans had moved to northern industrial cities to escape the impact of this "constitutional" discrimination and to find work other than that of itinerant sharecroppers and docile servants. Yet with this massive migration came feelings of displacement for many of those who were former slaves and for the sons and daughters of those slaves. This displacement was a symptomatic reaction to the new social climate. While the African Americans were now free men and women in the North, their freedom often took the form of a self-imposed isolationism, perhaps a vestige of their marginalization as a culture in the antebellum South. It is this sense of displacement, particularly but not exclusively of black males, which is dramatized in several ways in Wilson's play: in the "religiomagical" plantation dance, the juba; in what will be referred to as Zonia's song; in Wilson's inclusion of the blues song "Joe Turner's Come and Gone"; and especially in the central characters, Bynum Walker and Herald Loomis. Wilson states: "From the outset he [Loomis] has been a man who has suffered spiritual dislocation and is searching for a world that contains his image. The years of bondage to Joe Turner have disrupted his life and severed his connection to the past."[1]

Langston Hughes, Wilson's literary predecessor from the 1920s Harlem Renaissance, looks toward a longed-for but dimly perceived African heritage in works such as "The Negro Speaks of Rivers" and "Afro American Fragment." The following lines from Hughes's "Afro American Fragment" reveal an African continuum, a linkage to an African past that restores cultural pride in black Americans[2]

Subdued and time-lost are the drums—
And yet, through some vast mist of race
There comes this song
I do not understand
The song of atavistic land,
Of bitter yearnings lost, without a place—

So long,
So far away
Is Africa's
Dark face.[3]

Likewise Wilson, influenced by the Black Nationalist Movement of the 1960s, calls forth his African ancestors' cultural practices in stories, blues songs, echoing field-worker and railroad
songs, and dance. In *Joe Turner's Come and Gone* the significance of an individual's "song," and, in turn, African Americans' collective sense of displacement—a fragmented sense of
self and of community within America—is mitigated when the
central character Herald Loomis recalls his ancestral connection
to Africa. This "song of [an] atavistic land" is captured in the
juba, a dance that routinely begins after Sunday suppers in Seth
and Bertha Holly's boardinghouse. The boarders' participation
in the dance evokes Loomis's surrealistic vision of a people's
barbarous captivity, displacement, and virtual destruction. As
theater critic Jack Kroll points out, both the character of Loomis
and the juba play important roles in the conflict and development of the play: "The dreams, quests, hopes and fears of all the
characters interweave in a web of black fatality. It's the mysteri-
ous Loomis who finally rips the web apart, leaving everyone
freer to pursue their personal variation in the theme of freedom.
That freedom becomes visible in a shared *juba* dance, a signal
that these blacks will never be free until they accept and build
on their African heritage."[4]

In Wilson's play the juba signifies the recurrence (in memories, in deeds, and in visions) of remote ancestral ties—a pater-

nal, cultural legacy from the characters' African forefathers. Yet as scholarship on this subject indicates, the juba's origins and the interpretations surrounding the motivation for its practice are somewhat difficult to delineate. For example, Beverly J. Robinson analyzes one possible origin of the dance: "One of the earliest records of the term *juba* dates back to American minstrelsy. Both Juba and Jube consistently appeared as names of enslaved Africans who were skilled musicians and dancers. The father of a celebrated black artist who was popular outside the minstrelsy circuit, Horace or Howard Weston, was named Jube."[5] Robinson elaborates upon the myriad etymological origins of the word *juba: juba* or *diuba* in Bantu, which literally translated means "to pat, beat time, the sun, the hour." Linguistically the word *juba* comes from the African *giouba* referring to a sacred polyrhythmic African step dance whose secular origins trace back to South Carolina and the West Indies, where the word referred to both a mixture of leftovers consumed by the plantation slaves and a song that they created to prepare them psychologically to eat what Robinson calls "slop."[6]

If the reader of Wilson's play considers the following explication of the term in the *Oxford English Dictionary,* the cause of Herald Loomis's mental breakdown (or epiphany) and the juba's purgative effect upon him become clear. The *OED* defines *juba,* sometimes spelled "juber" or "jouba," as a species of dance that often included the reenactment of a mental breakdown. It was performed by the antebellum plantation slaves in the Deep South—a dance whose choreography consisted of the clapping of hands, the patting of knees and thighs, the striking of feet on the floor, and the singing of a refrain in which the word *juba* was repeated, a refrain that acted as an incantation to the Holy Ghost or an invocation to manifest a transcendent being.

Certainly, this mode of call-and-response communication was the only vehicle to voice a sense of community—not unlike the call-and-response spirituals that were sung by slaves on one plantation to communicate with those on another nearby plantation—in an environment where a sense of community was systematically undermined by the institution of slavery. In the same way, Bynum Walker as the Afrocentric spiritual healer in the play leads the disillusioned Herald Loomis through a series of questions to recall his African identity.

When the audience encounters the character of Herald Loomis, whose paroxysmal breakdown is prompted by his adverse reaction to the other characters' participation in the dance, it is initiated into a world in which the natural and supernatural coexist and impinge upon one another; as Loomis says to Walker: "The ground's starting to shake. There's a great shaking. The world's busting half in two. The sky's splitting open. I got to stand up."[7] The juba—as song, as dance, with all its competing cultural resonances—plays a significant role in Wilson's play. In the final scene of act 1 the residents of the boarding-house converse after Sunday dinner, except for Herald Loomis, who is not there. As they retire to the parlor, Seth and Jeremy want to juba, and the two wake Bynum Walker to join them in the dance. Instantly, the atmosphere is jubilant as the others join in. Then Loomis enters and cries out for them to stop. He blasphemes the Holy Ghost, the greatness of God's grandeur, and then unzips his pants. All are devastated as Loomis suddenly begins to speak in tongues and dance frenetically around the kitchen. Without a moment's hesitation Walker runs after him while Seth shouts out that Loomis is crazy and Bertha tells her husband to be quiet. Thrown back during his juba, Loomis tells of a horrific vision: bones walking upon the water, bones sinking into the depths of the water, and bones washing up upon the land where they transform into flesh, black flesh. Walker attempts to crawl closer to Loomis, and Loomis, who is nearly out of breath, tries to but cannot stand. Loomis knows that he must stand up to break the spell of this vision; he says that he must "get upon the road" like the others, but cannot and collapses onto the floor.

In the stage directions for this scene Wilson describes particularities of the juba and compares it to Herald Loomis's disturbing reaction to all those involved in the dance:

> *The Juba is reminiscent of the Ring Shouts of the African slaves. It is a call and response dance. BYNUM sits at the table and drums. He calls the dance as others clap their hands, shuffle and stomp around the table. It should be as African as possible, with performers working themselves up into a near frenzy. The words can be improvised, but should include some mention of the Holy Ghost. In the middle of the dance HERALD LOOMIS enters.*

LOOMIS: (*In a rage.*) Stop it! Stop it! (*They stop and look to him.*) You all sitting up here singing about the Holy Ghost? You singing and singing. You think the Holy Ghost is coming? You sing for the Holy Ghost to come? What he gonna do, huh? He gonna come with tongues of fire to

burn up your woolly heads? You gonna tie onto the Holy
Ghost and get burned up? What you got then? Why God
got to be so Big? Why he got to be bigger than me? How
much big is there? How much big do you want? (*LOOMIS
starts to unzip his pants.*) (52)

What disturbs Herald Loomis about the characters' participation in the dance is that sense of community, of solidarity, of an
atavistic legacy of Africa and sadly of the bondage still in the
consciousness of the post–Civil War generation, all of which are
in sharp contrast to his desire for autonomy. Why do they laud it
over him? Why do they wish to be reminded of their cultural
past? Is the dance and all that it represents more important than
an individual's efforts to become American? In an interview with
Richard Pettengill, Wilson revealed that *Joe Turner* is his favor-
ite play "because it was a symbolic resurrection of those Africans who were lost, tossed overboard during the Middle Passage,
and whose bones right now still rest at the bottom of the Atlantic
Ocean."[8] But some African Americans over the years have not
shared Wilson's sentiment on this issue.

Ronald Takaki writes that most blacks of the post–Civil War
generation walked away from anything that recalled their servitude in the South, "the racial etiquette of deference and subordination." Takaki claims that many who traveled north were
"restless, dissatisfied, unwilling to mask their true selves and
accommodate to traditional roles."[9] The juba , therefore, in Herald Loomis's mind re-establishes a connection to an unwanted
past and tradition that is unbearable and dangerous. Takaki says
that "compared to the 'older class of colored labor,' men who

were 'pretty well up in years' and who constituted a 'first rate class of labor,' the blacks of the 'younger class' were 'discontented and wanted to be roaming.'"[10]

When Herald Loomis tells Bynum Walker of his vision, he describes a wave that transforms the bones of their ancestors into flesh. Once he mentions this transformation, Herald Loomis's desperate desire for individual autonomy is reiterated: "'They got flesh on them! Just like you and me. . . . They black. Just like you and me. . . . They just laying there. . . . I got to stand up. I can't lay here no more. All the breath coming into my body and I got to stand up'" (54–55). Upon hearing this apostasy, Walker quickly recognizes that Loomis is a victim of his years of bondage to Joe Turner:"'See, Mr. Loomis, when a man forgets his song he goes off in search of it . . . till he find out he's got it with him all the time. That's why I can tell you one of Joe Turner's niggers.'Cause you forgot how to sing your song'" (71).

Walker sees that the traces of enslavement in Loomis's vision are a form of personal hegemony in which the song of the individual—that is, the individual's ties to the past as well as place in the world—is negated, and such was the goal of Joe Turner: "'What he wanted was your song. . . . Every nigger he catch he's looking for the one he can learn that song from. Now he's got you bound up to where you can't sing your own song. . . . But you still got it. You just forgot how to sing it'" (73). During this scene the others present seem aware of their autonomy as individuals apart from their identity as a race. They can participate in this dance as a form of celebration, for they can acknowledge their songs (words and actions) as signatures of their autonomy as individuals and as members of a race in this "act of tribal solidarity and recognition of communal history."[11] All can embrace this legacy of their culture both of Africa and America, but Herald Loomis cannot because of his haunting "Joe Turner" nightmare of imprisonment.

Although the same atavistic "ghost" is within him, Loomis believes that his autonomy as an individual, as a man, is at best tenuous. In an interview, Wilson explained the haunting presence of the white plantation owner from Tennessee and its effect upon the African American male: "Joe Turner would press Blacks into peonage. He would send out decoys who would lure Blacks into crap games and then he would sweep down and grab them. He had a chain with forty links to it, and he would take Blacks off to his plantation and work them."[12]

According to William W. Cook, the direct result of the institution of slavery upon African Americans was a deprivation of the coadunate elements within their native African culture. Consequently the practice of religions, languages, and customs became convergent and were expressed in art. He states that the African descended from an "absorptive culture, meaning a culture in which certain divisions do not exist."[13] Cook further elaborates that within an "absorptive culture" that implements the call and response pattern there is no line drawn between performer and audience as there is in Western theater and that words and dance are of equal importance as in the juba or as the vocals and instrument are in the blues. Therefore, in the play, when Herald Loomis attempts to stop the juba, he disrupts this call and response pattern, this cultural tradition, something which was not tolerated in African societies: "African societies discourage face-to-face confrontations and pull in line those who were out of line. This vent of feelings obviates the possibility that private grievances will fester and become a community problem. The great and powerful are in a sense leveled with the weak."[14]

Moreover, the juba—or, in general, African ritual dance— is "earth oriented," an expression of a kinship with the earth. This kinship is initially demonstrated in act 1 during the sacrificial ritual enacted by Bynum Walker near the Hollys' vegetable garden. In contrast, the choreographic movements of classical or European dance reflect a pull away from the earth, according to Cook. Therefore, Herald Loomis, being a member of the post– Civil War generation, attempts to sever that native African connection to the earth and to break free from that past connection to this "Joe Turner" enslavement in order to become Americanized in the post–Emancipation Proclamation America.

For amid what Herald Loomis perceives as a conspiratorial group, he degrades his own ancestry with his vociferous attack against the religiomagical elements of his African American ethnicity, including remarks about physical and sexual stereotypes to further his insult upon others present. And, even though he and Bynum Walker have an oral exchange, they are not engaging in "dozens"—a contest of call-and-response verbal combat highly regarded as a skill in African societies—because his oral attack is against the culture and results in his breakdown and collapse.

In Wilson's play an acute displacement, which is actually the African Americans' disfranchisement in white America, is reflected in each character's desire to participate in the synergistic juba—a dance of cultural mutability in America and of traditional immutability from their atavistic land. That disfranchisement is further illustrated in some of the key male characters' need to wander or to turn away from that which is familiar—hence, causing the "Joe Turner syndrome," a cultural idiom that refers both to the convict-lease system devised as a post-Reconstruction socioeconomic advantage allowing white southern landowners to further exploit black labor as well as the institution of slavery. The central characters are in search of their voice, a "song" that will enable them to articulate their individual and cultural identities, a song that, perhaps, will lead them down the "right road" and not down the behavioral road to aversion, a song that signifies these feelings of displacement, which are referred to as "Joe Turner."

Beyond its direct reference to enslavement, "Joe Turner" is a blues song that alludes to the African Americans' sense of imprisonment in a white world, a song Bynum Walker sings in the play:

They tell me Joe Turner's come and gone
Ohhh Lordy
They tell me Joe Turner's come and gone
Ohh Lordy
Got my man and gone

Come with forty links of chain
Ohhh Lordy
Come with forty links of chain
Ohh Lordy
Got my man and gone (67).

According to Amiri Baraka, African Americans' place in postslave society was nonexistent because the only role that they knew and that white America knew for them was on the periphery as slaves, even in the new "separate but equal" America: "Blues did begin in slavery, and it is from that 'peculiar institution,' as it is known euphemistically, that the blues did find its particular form. And if slavery dictated certain aspects of blues form and content, so did the so-called Emancipation and its subsequent problems dictate the path blues would take."[15] Essentially the blues reflects that displacement and engenders an African American vision, or, as Amiri Baraka claims, a legal subterfuge of their role as disfranchised Americans in this new free America—the America in August Wilson's *Joe Turner's Come and Gone*—where antebellum sentiments have not been erased.

Houston A. Baker, Jr., has explored the importance of the blues in the African American experience and has concluded that the blues are as difficult to define as the cultural experience of African Americans: "Afro-American blues constitute . . . a vibrant network. . . . in which Afro-American cultural discourse is inscribed."[16] As Baker explains, if readers look for a fixed meaning, the text of song and culture will semantically erupt through the process of interpretation. This complex, culturally inscribed discourse that informs the blues is apparent in Wilson's play. It is a cultural discourse that entails Christian elements alongside native African nature religious elements, a discourse that entails a longing for family and a sense of belonging as well as the desire to wander, and a discourse that entails the opportunities and obligations of freedom in conjunction with the lingering traces of slavery.

Some in Wilson's cast of characters reflect these complexities as well as the issue of displacement and the difficulties arising from attempts at acculturation. Even some of the characters' names exemplify their internal and external struggles. The Hollys' longtime boarder is Bynum Walker, a man who often speaks in parables and whose surname epitomizes the wanderer, the Joe Turner type. Walker is a man in his early sixties described as a rootworker: a conjure man who is known as "the Binding Man," for he is the glue that sticks everyone together or, more precisely, those who wish to be bound. Bynum Walker is described as the voodoo, heebee jeebee, mumbo jumbo, rootman who is looking for the shiny man. Walker, like his late father, has special powers. And, like his father before him, a plantation shaman who was known as the "Healing Man," Walker is the boarding-house's resident shaman. In fact, Walker's purpose, his song, lies in both his names: "Bynum," the one who binds people together so that they discover a sense of truth within themselves; "Walker," the one who wanders, a seeker.

Similar to those characters in the stories of Charles Chesnutt such as "The Goophered Grapevine" and "The Conjurer's Revenge," Bynum Walker embodies a strong sense of separateness between the world of the African American and that of the European American, for example, Rutherford Selig. Selig, "the People Finder," is a descendant of those who captured, bound, and enslaved Africans who appear in Loomis's horrific vision. He is the European American trickster, an amicable con man who transports blacks for a fee and then charges other blacks to locate them. His father was a man who captured escaped slaves for money, and his grandfather was a man who captured and transported slaves aboard ship for money. And Bertha notes that Selig is no different from his ancestors: "You can call him a People Finder if you want to. I know Rutherford Selig carries people away too. . . . Folks plan on leaving plan by Selig's timing. . . . Then he charge folks a dollar to tell them where he took them. . . . This old People Finding business is for the birds. He ain't never found nobody he ain't took away" (42).

Bynum Walker has binding skills of another kind. He is endowed with a powerful insight into the human condition, as his clairvoyant interpretation of Herald Loomis's vision—in which Loomis envisions bones with black flesh arising from the sea—indicates. And ultimately Walker's skills will lead to the reunion of Herald Loomis, Zonia, and Martha Pentacost Loomis in the play's final scene.

Walker also performs conjurations, or "goophers," in his rituals with the blood of pigeons and with curative concoctions, such as the one he gives to the heartbroken Mattie Campbell, to enable himself and others to overcome the sociological and psychological difficulties in an arbitrary white world. For example, Bertha Holly, a churchgoer who nevertheless expresses a faith in folk beliefs, respects Walker for his shamanistic or spiritual powers. She is not perturbed by Bynum Walker's mumbo jumbo and, more than tolerating him, defends Walker against Seth's mockery in the opening scene: "You don't say nothing when he bless the house . . . Seth, leave that man alone" (2). Bertha's response to Walker exemplifies this separation between the African American and the European American even further in that she can incorporate both elements of Christian (European) and African religions. Even though she practices the Christian religion, she sprinkles the boardinghouse with salt and lines pennies across the threshold to ward off evil spirits.

Throughout the play Bynum Walker is looking for the "shiny man," a modern-day shaman, and to assist him in that search, he requests the services of Rutherford Selig. On the road one day, Walker met the shiny man, who seemed hungry and lost, but the shiny man had a "voice" in his head that told him where to go. And that man said that he would reveal to Walker the "Secret of Life."

To Selig, Walker recalls his mystical journey with this man on the road, who, Walker says, initially paused at the bend and then told Walker to rub his hands together. When Walker did so, his hands began to secrete blood, which he was told to rub all over his body in order to "clean" himself. Herald Loomis performs a similar act at the end of the play when he slashes his chest and rubs the blood on his face. At this moment Loomis is freed from his ties to Joe Turner and, in contrast to his inability to stand after his vision in act 1, is able to stand on his own. Wilson reveals the importance of Loomis's epiphany in the stage directions: "*Having found his song, the song of self-sufficiency, fully resurrected, cleansed and given breath, free from any encumbrance other than the workings of his own heart and the bonds of the flesh, having accepted the responsibility for his own presence in the world, he [Loomis] is free to soar above the environs that weighed and pushed his spirit into terrifying con-*

*tractions*" (94). Herald Loomis then becomes the shiny man that Bynum Walker has been searching for so long, "shining like new money!"

Bynum's father appears during this journey: his stature was normal, but his mouth was enormous, and his hands as big as hams. The importance of his words are accentuated by the size of his mouth, and the size of his hands illustrates the impact of his paternal guidance. Sandra G. Shannon suggests that Bynum's description of his father and the place are intentionally hyperbolic in order to emphasize the mystical and allegorical qualities of his tale, "remarkably reminiscent of the African folktale."[17] The father grieves for his son who dwells in a world where he carries other people's songs around, not having a song of his own, and tells Walker that if he ever encounters a shiny man again, he will know that his song has served its purpose and he can die a happy man; Bynum will be a man who has left his mark on life, not just one of those marked men.

The word *mark* is significant, for the motif of "mark" in various contexts is explored throughout the play: "marked men and women" (xvii); "mark out" (3); "mark on life" (10); "marked man" (71); "mark down life" (71); "Joe Turner done marked me" (71); "got a mark on me" (71); "you mark what I'm saying" (74); and "made them marks" (79). Essentially this word and its meanings refer to the struggle of the African Americans with the status quo, the struggle of those "marked" who, like Cain, are banished from the chosen people.

There must be an antagonist in the play, but this antagonist is, ironically, the protagonist, an ex-convict appropriately named Herald Loomis. He will become the *Herald,* the shiny man, the one who knows all that came before as the ghost of Walker's father foretold. It appears, though, that Herald Loomis possesses a looming quality and is perceived by all others—with the exception of Zonia, his daughter, and Bynum Walker, his fellow boarder—as someone threatening, a menace. Even his attire, a long dark wool coat and hat, is ominous. When any character sees Loomis's face, Loomis is always described as wild-eyed and mean-looking. However, most of the characters, even Reuben Scott, know that Loomis is distraught because he cannot find his wife, Martha Pentecost Loomis, who has been gone nearly ten years.

Loomis's vision of the world and of himself is at odds with reality. At times, he claims that he is a deacon of a church and at times claims he had previously worked on a farm. Whether he is a deacon or farm laborer or both as he claims, or a gambler or a murderer as others speculate, and whether this farm is a prison farm on which he was a leased convict or a family farm that he maintained with his wife Martha, these aspects of Loomis's narrative are left somewhat suspect in Wilson's play. Undoubtedly, these elements in his story must remain suspect for Wilson to accentuate Loomis's internal struggle over his identity, as the character's dream or nightmare demonstrate. It seems that Loomis is an unwilling, self-imposed Joe Turner, despite the fact that he cannot understand the significance of his vision until Walker interprets it. In many ways, Herald Loomis as the shiny man, whom Bynum Walker has sent Selig to locate, is the blind prophet who sees more than he knows, as Bynum Walker eventually will discover.

Despite the fact that "August Wilson has apparently chosen to focus on the African American man's oppression in this country to symbolize the collective struggles of all African American males," as Sandra G. Shannon asserts, some of Wilson's female characters find their own salvation, their sense of identity.[18] Bynum Walker explains the significance of a woman to Jeremy Furlow: "'When you grab hold to a woman, you got something there. . . . When your [*sic*] hold to that woman and look at the whole thing and see what you got . . . why, she can take and make something out of you'" (45).

One of the most significant female characters in Wilson's play is Zonia Loomis. Her unique rendition of the blues, as voiced by a child on the verge of adolescence, is encoded with what Baker calls "the amalgam" of purposes of the blues. Her songs represent the "always becoming, shaping, transforming, displacing the peculiar experience of Africans in the New World."[19] Zonia represents a mark of intersection, Loomis's vehicle to interact with other characters, and, in turn, she acts as a guide into her father's enigmatic character. The following is an excerpt from the song that Zonia sings:

> Tomorrow, Tomorrow
> Tomorrow never comes
> The marrow the marrow
> The marrow in the bone. (27)

This entire song describes Loomis's departure from his life with his wife Martha, from his labor on Henry Thompson's farm, and from reality into a phantasmagoric self-imposed exile. This exile led Loomis inevitably to his incessant atavistic vision, such as the one in the parlor during the juba, of the Africans' horrific journey to America and the African Americans' experience in America, which is reflected in the line "the marrow and the bone."

Wilson says that the allusion to bones spiritually connects Loomis to his ancestors, the "bones people."[20] It is not until Loomis can confront his own demons that his nontemporal state of limbo, or "tomorrow never comes" attitude, can change.

The lines to this song are also emblematic of Zonia's relationship with her father, for she must accompany him on his travels in search of Martha. Zonia wants to remain Loomis's little girl forever. Despite the fact that she is growing up, Zonia attempts to remain small and slight, "a spider," even at eleven years old. Zonia realizes that one day they will find Martha and that she will have to stay with her mother forever. Her interaction with Reuben Scott, the little boy who lives near the boardinghouse, exemplifies her dream that things remain the same, that "tomorrow never comes." Zonia's song, then, is about her life.

Reuben Scott, who lives with his grandfather next door to the boardinghouse, clings to the past as well. Reuben sizes up others according to his grandfather's criteria and constantly asks why Zonia is there, to which she replies that someone named Joe Turner did something wrong to her father which caused her mother to leave them abruptly. Reuben and Zonia are kindred spirits. Zonia is deeply fond of her father, never wants to leave his side, and wants to stay his little girl forever. Reuben refuses to relinquish his relationship with his dead friend by keeping the pigeon coop as a sort of a shrine. Both children try to hold on to the past, Zonia through her behavior and Reuben through the pigeon coop.

While Zonia dreads and longs to put off that day when she will have to start her life anew, Mattie Campbell sees such new beginnings as a recurring and inescapable aspect of life, as she tells Herald Loomis: "I ain't never found no place for me to fit. Seem like all I do is start over. It ain't nothing to find no starting place in the world. You just start from where you find yourself" (76). Mattie Campbell is one female character who represents a composite portrait of the dissolution of a myth—the socially inscribed, traditional roles to which all African America women had unwillingly acquiesced. Mattie meets Jack Carper, a Joe Turner, in Texas while picking peaches with her mother, who dies before Mattie moves in with Carper. Carper leaves because he considers Mattie to be a cursed woman, a postlapsarian Eve. Consequently Mattie moves north and into the Hollys' boardinghouse, eventually moving in with Jeremy Furlow, a man who has been conditioned by his brief encounters with those he meets at work on the road crew, at the local bar, or at the boardinghouse. Of course, Furlow will leave Mattie too, and she will linger on the hope that someday Carper will return—until Bynum Walker tells her otherwise. What is interesting about Mattie's character is that she rushes out the door after Herald Loomis at the end of the play because both characters at that moment come to the realization that tomorrow does come and that people do, or can, change.

Three of the female characters—Zonia, Mattie, and even Martha—represent the dissolution of a myth—a simplified, traditional, dichotomous portrait of women as merely doting mothers or conniving Mata Haris. Simply stated, each woman is psychologically complex. They are black female migrants in search of their own songs, a sense of spiritual and emotional stability in their lives. Each woman's interaction with the Joe Turners, those disfranchised African Americans males, elicits a change to some extent within each one of them, resulting in a song of self that each woman must discover for herself.

Thus August Wilson clearly addresses the issue of uprooted African Americans, for they as a culture have been "enslaved" both physically and psychologically. The need to dispel or shake off an identity as a nonman (or nonperson) is an important theme in this play, which has been described as a panoramic and insightful view of black America and a spiritual allegory. Wilson describes his view of the African American experience in this way: "My generation of blacks knew very little about the past of our parents. . . . They shielded us from the indignities that they suffered."[21] Although he was shielded from them while growing up, the indignities Wilson mentions are nonetheless a part of the African American's experience.

When asked to define his role in the theater, Wilson identifies himself as a "cultural nationalist [a playwright who is] trying to raise consciousness through theater."[22] Wilson's play must and does contain complex themes and complex characters. To a varying extent Bynum Walker, Herald Loomis, Mattie Campbell, and Zonia Loomis each experiences his or her own private purgation, a sense of displacement or disfranchisement, which each character expresses through song. Whether this song is the juba, a blues song such as "Joe Turner's Come and Gone," or a voice to express his or her troubles, each character's song enables him or her to find strength, to begin his or her life anew, and, for August Wilson, to leave the "mark" of African American culture on the American stage.

# CHAPTER FIVE

# *The Piano Lesson*

In the fashion of Greek epics in which warriors anticipate the onslaught of their rivals in battle, Wilson's *The Piano Lesson* begins at dawn. Boy Willie Charles encroaches upon his sister Berniece's territory, the Charles household, and the two will soon engage in a battle of wills over their legacy, an intricately carved piano. In the stage directions Wilson foreshadows this battle: "The lights come up on the Charles household. It is five o'clock in the morning. The dawn is beginning to announce itself, but there is something in the air that belongs to the night. A stillness that is portent, a gathering, a coming together of something akin to a storm. There is a loud knock on the door."[1] Boy Willie enters with his friend Lymon, and both are greeted by Boy Willie's uncle Doaker, a middle-aged railroad cook. It seems that the truck Boy Willie and Lymon used to transport watermelons from Mississippi to Pittsburgh is in disrepair. On the surface Boy Willie's intention is to visit the relatives, but actually, as he soon discloses, the true intention of his visit is to secure the family piano and sell it. The battle over the piano, its meaning as both legacy and opportunity, and the choices all the key characters make comprise the central conflict of *The Piano Lesson.*

Throughout the play, the piano stands on the stage as a silent testament to American racism while the various characters wandering in and out of the parlor testify to their experiences. The play's central symbol is the piano, and the conflict over its possession is just as important as the interwoven narratives it calls forth. The physical disturbance of Boy Willie's arrival awakens Berniece, but his presence in the house, physically and symbolically, also seems to awaken the dead. Boy Willie announces that Sutter, whose land he intends to purchase and whose brother he intends to visit in Chicago, was found drowned in a well on his property. This drowning is not unusual because there have been reports of other mysteriously accidental drowning victims as well. Boy Willie exclaims that many say that the Ghosts of Yellow Dog are to blame, the vengeful spirits of four black men—including Boy Charles, Boy Willie, and Berniece's father—who were burned alive in a boxcar aboard the Yellow Dog railroad line on July 4, 1911, by a few white townsfolk at the behest of Sutter's father, Robert Sutter, purportedly for stealing the piano. This is one reason, Doaker later informs Boy Willie, that Berniece will never let him sell the piano. It is the Charles family's legacy. Even Avery Brown—the local preacher and her prospective husband, or so Avery believes—has been unsuccessful in his attempt to persuade Berniece to sell the piano.

No one from the Charles family except Doaker is fully aware of the connection between the Sutter and the Charles family and of the struggle over possession of this piano. However, this connection lies dormant in the consciousness of Berniece and Boy Willie, hovering between the past and the present. That past is brought to life and commemorated through the various characters' stories. But the past is also alive in the form of Sutter's ghost, who stalks through Berniece's house. Soon after Boy Willie's arrival, Berniece is heard shouting for Doaker; she sees Sutter's ghost at the top the stairs. Berniece says that the ghost is looking for Boy Willie. In utter disbelief, Boy Willie assumes that Berniece is delusional and Sutter a figment of her imagination. Adamantly, Berniece asks Boy Willie and Lymon to leave, for they will bring nothing but trouble. Boy Willie refuses to leave, and Berniece insinuates that Boy Willie pushed Sutter into the well and then mentions Crawley, her late husband whom she loved. To Berniece, Boy Willie is responsible for Crawley's tragic demise. Clearly, the conflict between brother and sister has a history all its own, but Berniece and Boy Willie also represent two different attitudes toward history, two different responses to the past and its relationship to the present.

As Alan Nadel points out, "Berniece, we could say, wants to hide from history and Boy Willie wants to get rid of it. Wilson, however, wants to rewrite it, even if he has to use traditionally white instruments, even if he has to resurrect some ugly ghosts, for the alternative, it would seem, is to deny African Americans their art and their history."[2] Beyond this, Wilson forces white America onto the stage as well, but not the version or images of history that white Americans would prefer to recall or portray in their own stories. Wilson simultaneously portrays both the lingering trauma of slavery and its scars on African Americans while rendering mute and absent the white presence on stage, allowing him to foreground instead the personal stories of his characters.

For example, early in the play Boy Willie initiates one of Doaker's stories by saying that the women in Mississippi want Doaker to return. Doaker responds by telling his story and providing more history of the Charles family. For twenty-seven years Doaker has been working for the railroad. When Boy Willie was a toddler, his mother used to boast about his uncle. Before Doaker was a cook, he laid track for the Yellow Dog trainline. Wining Boy, Boy Willie and Berniece's uncle, an unsuccessful musician and gambler, worked for a while, about six months, until he succumbed to playing music and gambling. As Doaker continues to tell Boy Willie and Lymon about his life on the railroad, he imparts his philosophy of life as well by relating the stories of the passengers he has seen.

Toward the end of the nineteenth century railroads crept across the landscape of the South, and to many they provided a means to escape the racial oppression of the South. For Wilson, underlying individual stories such as Doaker's—of trains, tracks, schedules, and passengers—is the larger story of the Great Migration of African Americans who attempted to reach their final destination, to discover the place they could call home. The problem for these southern blacks, according to Doaker, was that in their desperation to change the direction of their lives, their ignorance of what lay ahead often led to disaster. Disfranchisement, in its many manifestations, was commonplace in both the South and the North. Thus, the train represents the hope of opportunity and change as well as the despair, failure, and loss that often follow hope.

Wilson employs the metaphor of a train in many of his plays to illustrate African Americans' unwillingness to settle for the inferior position of being third-class citizens in the confines of white America, even when the outcome of their journey was uncertain. In the character of Doaker, Wilson conveys optimism along this uncertain journey. Doaker believes that if one desires to change the direction of one's life, this change should begin at home. Seize the moment to implement political change at home first, then, as Doaker asserts, take that train and lay new tracks with the knowledge that change is also possible elsewhere: "Now you can start from anywhere. Don't care where you at. . . . if the train stays on the track . . . it's going to get you where it's going. If it ain't, then all you got to do is sit and wait cause the train's coming back to get you. The train don't never stop. It'll come back every time . . ." (18–19).

In the exchange over Doaker's description of his journey through life, the audience learns the purpose of Boy Willie's journey north: to stake claim to his legacy, the piano. Boy Willie's identity, albeit unconsciously, is engendered in this legacy. Invested within those carvings lies his identity as a black man. And Boy Willie views the acquisition of Sutter's land in a similar light. If he acquires that land or rides that train, so to speak, it will validate his existence as a free black man and put him on the right track, as an owner, not a slave like those ancestors represented in the carvings. By acquiring the land from the grandson, Boy Willie will psychologically usurp the power of the grandfather, the slave master who traded his and Berniece's great-grandmother and Doaker's father for the piano. And, on a grander scale, through his sale of the piano Boy Willie may redefine, or in part negate, the terrain and history of enslavement and racial oppression that still blocks him from realizing his version of the American Dream.

It is in Boy Willie's desire to seek his future and his fortune in the South that Kim Pereira sees a variation on a theme that dominates Wilson's earlier plays. In *Ma Rainey's Black Bottom, Fences,* and *Joe Turner's Come and Gone* "migration to the North is a major theme," but in *The Piano Lesson* the South for the first time is seen as a place that also offers opportunities to African Americans: "we are introduced to characters eager to return to the South. This is significant, for it marks a potential turning point in the fortunes of black people. Up to now, their search for their true identities—while ending in Africa—had been accompanied by journeys to the North, away from their farms and families. For the first time a character suggests the South as a place for them to pursue their destinies as free men and women."[3]

In contrast to Boy Willie, who in his way is still running from the past, Avery seems to have found his calling, his dream, and made strides toward it. Dressed in the attire of a preacher, Avery seems to have adapted well to the North. He tells Boy Willie and Lymon that he has obtained a job as an elevator operator at the Gulf Building in the city. Content with this menial service job, the aspiring preacher proudly extols the benefits of being gainfully employed, with such virtues as a pension plan and a turkey every Thanksgiving. Avery is glad that he no longer has to pick cotton the way he did in the South. Ironically Avery fails to comprehend that this job in the North is basically as prestigious as picking cotton in the South. In Avery's life the train is the dream, his calling and salvation, for it is his vehicle upon whose tracks he rides toward his destiny in life, impelling him to become a preacher. Yet Avery cannot find the home in which to make this vocation a reality until he secures a loan from the bank and establishes his church, the Good Shepherd Church.

Boy Willie is uninterested in Avery's calling; he even mocks the Christian rite of blessing the Charles Home with holy water when he hoists a pot of water and recites an incantation of his own to exorcize Sutter's ghost. All Boy Willie wants is the name of the white man who wants to buy the piano, which Avery cannot give him nor will his sister provide. Absurdly he tells Doaker that he will cut the piano in two. Since both he and Berniece view the piano as a legacy of their birthright, he feels justified. With this statement Wilson evokes in his audience a biblical parallel to King Solomon's solution as a means to foreshadow the resolution between these two disgruntled siblings at the play's conclusion.

As act 1 continues, Wining Boy, Boy Willie and Berniece's uncle, a former musician and gambler, tells the story of the Ghosts of Yellow Dog and their connection to the Charles family history. It is one marred by the indifference of the white man, but also the family is vindicated by the retribution of the Ghosts of Yellow Dog, as the litany of the ghosts' victims suggests. Wining Boy says if anyone wants proof beyond these acts of retribution, they can go to where the Southern and the Yellow Dog railroads intersect and call out the ghosts' names, and they will talk back. Lymon only perpetuates Wining Boy's belief by saying that he has heard that one can ask them questions as well. This story of the Ghosts of Yellow Dog provides a stimulus for Lymon to tell of his brush with the law down south.

After Boy Willie and Lymon fled from the law when Crawley was killed, the sheriff found Lymon and put him in jail. Stoval paid one hundred dollars to secure Lymon's release from jail, with the stipulation that Lymon work for him. Rather than work for Stoval, Lymon fled to the North. He assumed that up north the black man was treated better than he was in the South. Boy Willie says that Lymon's faith in the North is misdirected, for whites "treat you like you let them treat you," no matter where it occurs (38). Boy Willie's observation is correct in that it summarizes the experience of African Americans and the recurring views of the Wilson hero. Uncertainty prevails, for their journey might lead them to a new life filled with hope, or it might lead them to dread and death.

Wining Boy affirms Boy Willie's assessment of Lymon's predicament, but only goes so far. Wining Boy tells of a black man arrested for picking berries. This black man is innocent because he unknowingly picked berries on a white man's property that had no fence to mark its borders. Thus, the stories these characters relay to one another about their past experiences indicate that borders are established, defined, and dictated by the white man's territorial prerogative. And in the cases of both property and law the white man is somehow empowered whereas the black man is always somehow victimized. Wining Boy's story suggests that owning property and defining its borders corresponds with the power of the law to define who or what is right and who or what is wrong. Drawing borders, therefore, is an act of power that can both create and exclude, define and sever.

The white man's will and its dire consequences for the black man are also conveyed in folk beliefs. And in addition to the stories that these characters exchange about their encounters with white authority, they also trade tales about unusual encounters, ghosts and spirits, and folk explanations of uncommon events. Just like all the stories told by the various characters in Wilson's play, whether the Ghosts of Yellow Dog are real or imagined, they represent folk beliefs made manifest in the minds of these victims of white oppression in the South. These stories enable the characters to articulate their dissenting voices and to negotiate their way in a white world.

When Boy Willie asks Wining Boy to play a tune on the piano in order to dispel the thoughts of their mutual servitude on Parchman's farm, Wining Boy refuses because he is glad to be rid of the piano that has caused him tremendous grief. Wining Boy noticed that his identity began to merge with the piano; he simply became the piano player, an invisible one whose sole purpose was to entertain: "All you know how to do is play the piano. Now who am I? Am I me? Or am I the piano player? Sometime it seem like the only thing to do is shoot the piano player cause he is the cause of all the trouble I'm having" (41). After Wining Boy sadly recollects his relationship to the piano, an instrument that subsumed his identity as a man into the role of the musician, Doaker carefully recounts the story of Sutter and his relationship to the piano for Boy Willie. Sutter wants to claim the piano because it is a possession of his family, even though the carvings upon it were made by their great grandfather Willie Boy, Boy Willie's namesake. Willie Boy took the piano from Robert Sutter because inscribed in its wood is the Charles family's history.

Sutter's grandfather was Robert Sutter, who owned Willie Boy's family and purchased the piano from a man named Joel Nolander. The piano was to be an anniversary present for Robert Sutter's wife, Ophelia. Since Sutter was low on money at the time, he traded two of his slaves in exchange for the piano. Nolander selected Doaker's grandmother, also named Berniece, and his father, who was then just nine years old. Dependent upon these slaves, Ophelia wanted them back and offered to return the piano to Nolander in exchange. Devastated that the exchange was refused, Ophelia was heartbroken and fell ill. Unable to cope any longer with his wife's failing health, Sutter called upon Willie Boy, an accomplished woodcarver, to carve the likenesses of his wife and child in the wood. He did so and more. Willie Boy, through his carving, inscribed a totemic procession of their family history in the piano's wood. The workings of Willie Boy's imagination made manifest in wood delighted Ophelia so much that she played the piano until she died, but it angered Sutter. As much as the presence of the piano angered Sutter's ancestor, Doaker's brother—Berniece's and Boy Willie's father—Papa Boy Charles, the eldest of the three boys, thought of that piano often and wanted to take it away from Sutter family. To Boy Charles, the piano was a record of the Charles family history, replete with the joys they experienced and struggles they endured.

The reaction to Doaker's telling the Charles family history is mixed. Boy Willie utters that his father would have wanted to sell the piano as an act of retribution against the Sutter legacy of peonage. That is why later in act 1 Boy Willie asks Lymon to see if they can move the piano. But once they begin to move it, Doaker hears Sutter's ghost. Doaker is the only one who hears the ghost because he knows the piano rightfully belongs within the Charles home. To Boy Willie, the piano represents his economic mobility; the land is an invaluable investment in contrast to any sentimental attachment to the piano that Berniece may have. If Berniece gave lessons to pay the rent, that would be a different case, but she will not even touch its keys. Both siblings acknowledge that it cost their father his life, but Berniece remains steadfast in keeping the piano as a Charles family possession.

Berniece recognizes their mother's attachment to the piano, a sign of reverence to their father and, in turn, their forefathers. Unable to accept her brother's desire to sell the piano, Berniece suggests that Boy Willie, Papa Boy Charles, Wining Boy, and Doaker are nothing but thieves and killers. They are now and have always been selfish in their efforts to make their way in the world, and such attempts to secure better lives for themselves have always resulted in disastrous consequences such as Crawley's death. Crawley died in an altercation with some white men representing Jim Miller—Crawley, Boy Willie, and Lymon's white employer—over Boy Willie and Lymon stealing wood. While Crawley stayed and was killed, Boy Willie and Lymon fled, during which Boy Willie was shot in the stomach. Both Boy Willie and Lymon were later imprisoned, indentured on Parchman's farm, a prison camp, for their part in the incident. Boy Willie says Crawley was shot because he confronted the sheriff and others with a gun.

Act 1 has only two scenes to provide the play's necessary exposition, to present the various stories that collectively comprise the Charles family history and predicament. Act 2, in contrast, contains five seemingly truncated scenes to provide a staccato pace and heighten the suspense. In doing so, Wilson manages to complete the portrait of the Charles family and those whom they befriend and to reveal the family's need to resurrect the spirits of their ancestral past. Act 2 also offers a series of events that forces each member of the Charles family to face the legacy, the piano and its history, that until recently stood silently in Berniece's home.

*THE PIANO LESSON*

When act 2 begins, Doaker tells Wining Boy that Berniece is a cleaning woman for one of the city's wealthy steel executives and that Maretha, Berniece's daughter, is afraid to sleep upstairs now and that he had seen Sutter's ghost before Berniece did. Wining Boy says that they should never sell it and that he is not disturbed by the presence of Sutter's ghost. The mention of the ghost always signals the entrance of Boy Willie. Suddenly through the door the jovial Boy Willie and Lymon enter; they made much money selling their watermelons to the white folks in the neighborhood. The watermelons were selling so fast that Boy Willie inflated their price for more profit. Boy Willie even concocted a story about growing the watermelons in ground laden with sugar to assure a white customer of their sweetness. Boy Willie beams with satisfaction over this ingenious deceit and his ability to sell: "Them white folks is something else . . . ain't they, Lymon?" (59).

Ignorance or gullibility is not always attributed to the white oppressor, though. Stereotypes are further explored by Wilson when Lymon purchases the silk suit from the money-hungry Wining Boy, who cleverly present it as a kind of aphrodisiac bait to the woman-hungry Lymon. Afterward Lymon goes out for the evening to find women at a local movie theater, failing to comprehend that no woman will see him or the suit in the dark. As Wining Boy illustrates in his story about Lymon's family history, there are connections between the Charles family and Lymon's in many ways. The character of Lymon offers more than comic relief. Lymon's personal history is woven into the Charles family history. So, too, Lymon's history is representative of many black males, particularly regarding unlucky encounters with the law, women, and the supernatural.

Later in the play, though, impressed with himself in the suit, Lymon's smooth talking transforms Berniece's sullen disposition. But Lymon crosses Berniece's threshold for tolerance when he offers her the perfume that he was going to give to Dolly, a woman he met earlier that night. This gift takes Berniece off guard because she has not been in intimate contact with any man since Crawley. In the stage directions Wilson indicates that Berniece's kiss proves that Lymon, indeed, has the ability to mesmerize women even in Wining Boy's old silk suit. Maybe Lymon is not so unlucky after all.

The audience senses Berniece's difficulty in many of her relationships to men: romantic relationships with men such as Crawley and Avery and her sibling relationship with Boy Willie. Over the years Berniece has not only held onto the piano and guarded the family legacy, but has also held onto the pain of personal loss that her troubled relationships with men have caused. As Avery says: "What is you ready for, Berniece? You gonna drift along from day to day. Life is more than making it from one day to another. You gonna look up one day and it's all gonna be past you" (68). Both of these burdens have come to haunt Berniece and explain her reluctance and her anger. Wilson reveals the irreconcilable cohabitation of Christian beliefs with distinctly African American folk beliefs when Berniece, as a good Christian woman, suggests that Avery bestow a blessing upon the house to ward off the evil spirit of Sutter and later exorcizes the ghost in her own way.

Kim Marra offers an interesting assessment of Berniece's behavior that provocatively links her with Sutter's ghost: "Berniece not only exerts paradigmatic matriarchal dominance over the household, but presumes custody of the piano. Moreover, Wilson aligns her with forces of white oppression in withholding the piano from Boy Willie; every time Boy Willie tries to move the piano, Sutter's ghost becomes agitated along with Berniece. In keeping with black nationalist gender ideology, black matriarchy is shown to be complicit with white supremacy in the economic and sexual emasculation of the black male."[4] Marra's explanation of the conflict between these two siblings as, in part, revealing the complicity between black matriarchy and white supremacy in the sexual emasculation of the black man is seen in Berniece's confrontation with Boy Willie over his date with Grace. Berniece asserts her matriarchal prerogative in the Charles household and thereby prevents Boy Willie's sexual liaison with Grace in her home.

By refusing to leave, Boy Willie designates the parlor as a battleground and makes the first move. When the stage directions indicate that Boy Willie first draws an imaginary line across the floor with his foot, implying that he is no longer trespassing on Berniece's side of the house, Wilson invites the audience to witness Berniece's power of conviction to keep the piano in what is to be the beginning of their final confrontation. Berniece makes the next move with a threat of eternal damnation, only to hear her Christian beliefs slighted in Boy Willie's story of a puppy he lost and attempted to resurrect through earnest prayers to God, which leads to his discussion of her need to direct that faith toward the living, her daughter Maretha.

Boy Willie believes that Berniece should instill pride in Maretha by sharing the Charles family history etched in the carvings upon the piano. It is their history, and she should be proud to tell it her daughter the family story: "You ought to mark down on the calendar the day that Papa Boy Charles brought that piano into the house. You ought to mark that day down and draw a circle around it . . . and every year when it come up throw a party. . . . If you did that she wouldn't have no problem in life. She could walk around here with her head held high" (91). Ironically, he then tells the story of Papa Boy Charles, who worked another's land but never owned a single acre of it himself, and in the telling attempts to sever the piano from the future Charles family history. If Papa Boy Charles had had a chance like Boy Willie has now, he would have sold the piano; he would have felt proud to have owned a piece of land: "If you got a piece of land you'll find everything else will fall into place" (92). Through no fault of their own, life consisted of drudgery for Papa Boy Charles and Mama Ola, yet they did not wallow in despair. Boy Willie asks Berniece why she is creating a similar downtrodden environment for Maretha: "If you teach that girl that she's living at the bottom of life, she's gonna grow up and hate you" (92).

Berniece's response reveals much. She, as a cleaning woman, believes that all blacks are at the bottom of the social and economic ladder, and she conveys this belief in the form of hopelessness to Maretha. Boy Willie, therefore, tries to instill in his sister some of the hope she has lost. Berniece must accept that Crawley is gone, except in memory. Boy Willie, believing that Berniece's association with Avery has perpetuated such negative feelings, never concedes, negotiates, or surrenders to a subordinate position in his relationship with the white man unless there is no other option. Boy Willie addresses everyone in the parlor when he says he sees the benefits on the horizon: "I was born to a time of fire. So what I got to do? I got to mark my passing on the road. Just like you write on a tree, 'Boy Willie was here'" (93–94). It is this declaration of character that indicates Boy Willie's indomitable spirit to be his own master in the white man's world.

Throughout the play the heated conflict that arises between Berniece and Boy Willie occurs because Boy Willie has come to take possession of this family heirloom and sell it so that he can purchase a plot of land, a plot of land that signifies to Boy Willie his rightful piece of the American Dream. To Boy Willie the piano is the means to an end, the end being his ownership of the property: "I'm trying to get me some land, woman. I need that piano to get me some money so I can buy Sutter's land" (50). In contrast, to Berniece the piano is history, their history: "Money can't buy what that piano cost. You can't sell your soul for money . . ." (50). The piano is like a contract with the past, not to be negotiated, but maintained. Thus, understandably, Berniece is enraged by Boy Willie's blatant disregard of the ancestry which the piano represents to her, for the piano is a protonarrative of the Charles family history.

As the play reaches its conclusion, the audience overhears but does not witness the struggles between Boy Willie and Sutter's ghost, and Boy Willie is seen thrown to the bottom of the stairs repeatedly. The last time he ascends the stairs with frenzied determination, loud noises are heard from upstairs, and Berniece senses that she must play upon the piano's keys to exorcize Sutter's ghost. But Berniece's song does more than that, for in her playing "is found piece by piece . . . a song that is both a commandment and a plea. . . . It is intended as an exorcism and a dressing for battle. [It is a battle of historical and personal proportions for the Charles family.] A rustle of wind blowing over two continents" (106). And that is why the audience and those in the parlor hear the sound of an approaching train that signifies the passage, the long journey from the past to the present within the narrative context of the Charles family history. Now the ghost of Sutter is silenced at last.

The piano, in archaeological terms, is an artifact. From its carvings the Charles family and its future descendants can excavate the past, those silenced narratives appropriated pictorially upon its encasement. What angers Berniece is that Boy Willie sees the piano as an object rather than artifact and in doing so negates its personal and cultural value and abandons the role entrusted to members of the Charles family to preserve their history. What also angers Berniece is that the piano resurrects the pain that she associates with it, a pain so deep that she is unable to play upon its keys. Berniece begrudgingly reveals this fact to Avery: "I done told you that I don't play on that piano. Ain't no need in you to keep talking this choir stuff. When my mama died I shut the top on that piano and I ain't never opened it since. . . . I used to think them pictures came alive and walked through the house. Sometime late at night I could hear my mama taking to them. I said that wasn't gonna happen to me. I don't play that piano cause I don't want to wake them spirits. They never be walking around in this house" (70).

Although Boy Willie vituperatively remarks on numerous occasions that he views this legacy as a burden that he could eliminate by selling the piano, in this passage Berniece too admits its burden. When Berniece finally succumbs and touches the piano's keys, the loss of those whom she loved overwhelms her; she reawakens their spirits from the dead and thereby relinquishes the sorrow of the past and accepts the fact that she represents the continuation of that legacy, her blood line. As Doaker tells Boy Willie early in act 1, when Mama Ola died seven years earlier, Berniece refused to play because "She say it got blood on it . . ." (10). Berniece over the years has secured herself in her grief, and Boy Willie shatters her protective facade by attempting to take the piano. Thus, when she plays upon its keys, the battle over ownership is settled. The vanquished, Boy Willie, and the victor, Berniece, grow closer together with the expression of each note, which Wilson's stage directions at the beginning of the play portend: "a coming together of something akin to a storm . . ." (1). Amid the bout of sibling discord is a shared history, a provocation of history through blood rendered in the pictorial carving of ancestors that cannot be denied.

But the conclusion of *The Piano Lesson,* while seemingly resolving the conflict between Berniece and Boy Willie as well as between the past and present, raises some interesting questions. This resolution to the conflict, in fact, offers no resolution at all. Although Boy Willie and Berniece reconcile their exchange over the piano, Sutter's ghost can return to the Charles house in the future as easily as Boy Willie can, a fact that Boy Willie admits in his parting words. Much of the ambiguity stems from Wilson's attitude toward the play's resolution: "We had about five different endings to the play. But it was always the same ending: I wanted Boy Willie to demonstrate a willingness to battle with Sutter's ghost, the ghost of the white man—that lingering idea of him as the master of slaves—which is still in black Americans' lives and needs to be exorcized. I wasn't so much concerned with who ended up with the piano, as with Boy Willie's willingness to do battle."[5] Anne Fleche perceives the conclusion to the play as a musical interlude separating and distinguishing apparently irreconcilable opponents: "This grappling with the white ghost of the slave-owning past is symbolized as *voice* in Wilson's plays—as song, instrument, rhythm, style. And this voice, while it wrestles with the duality of black and white, past and present (or future), doesn't solve or obliterate these oppositions; it drives a wedge between them, keeping them *separate,* making distinctions—as at the end of *Piano Lesson,* when Sutter's ghost disappears but is not absorbed or destroyed."[6]

In an analysis of the play's conclusion Michael Morales describes the difference between an early version of the play used in performances and published in *Theater* and a later version performed on Broadway. As Morales explains, the song Berniece sings was originally a plea to the Christian God, but in the later version Berniece's call goes out to her ancestors, which strengthens the play's thematic ties to African ritual. For Morales, the consequence of this revision is that

the ghost of Sutter becomes the disembodied embodiment of the slaveholder's historical perspective (and perhaps even the dominant culture's control of history). This perspective is expelled from the community with the reestablishment of the kinship bond (the historical connection). In this respect, the expulsion of Sutter is a metaphor of historical self-definition for blacks in America. Inasmuch as this self-definition occurs through expelling the dominant culture's historical perspective, it is also an appeal for a separate history and separate historical institutions, necessitated by a cultural difference based upon a distinct narrative or origin and historical perspective.[7]

Perhaps the lesson of the play's conclusion is that there are indeed voices and perspectives that do not capitulate or fall prey to the dominant culture's version of history. In *The Piano Lesson* Wilson lets the audience know that those ancestral voices must be heard; otherwise they can paralyze, as they do in Berniece's case, or confound, as they do when Boy Willie attempts to overcome them with sheer brute force, and contribute to, throughout most of the play, the Charles family's disintegration instead of spiritual reconciliation.

# CHAPTER SIX

# *Two Trains Running*

In *Two Trains Running,* whose title comes from a Muddy Waters's blues song titled "Still a Fool," August Wilson explores the lives of African Americans whose sense of community is disrupted by the appearance of progress and whose prospects for procuring the American Dream are suspect in what is now a northern urban ghetto. Memphis Lee and the patrons of his restaurant stand on the precipice of urban renewal and must consider their prospects for survival and their loss of identity without their community once that community no longer exists. These characters' need to preserve their dignity has been mitigated or redefined by the desire to gamble, kill, self-mutilate, rob, or rage against the sources of their dissolution, whether external or internal. The external forces are often identified as those few whites from the present who dwell within this community or those many whites from the past who dwell outside of it—such as Lutz, Zanelli, Hartzberger, Hendricks, Mellon, Stovall, Boykins—all of whom have economic control over those who reside there. As a result, in one way or another these characters are searching for a means of salvation, a way to preserve their dignity, and a deliverance from the misfortune that has befallen them.

The time of *Two Trains Running* is 1969, after the assassination of Malcolm X, Martin Luther King, Jr., and Robert F. Kennedy. The Civil Rights Movement had been underway for sometime, but many African Americans continued to live in the same conditions they had for decades. The emotional and powerful speeches, the expressions of high ideals, the anticipated moments of social change that comprise the 1960s in many people's minds, are not the topics of Wilson's play. This play is about another 1960s, another history. Wilson focuses on a few African Americans, like many others, whose present does not differ all that much from their past. While West has gained quite a bit of financial success and Memphis gains some financial success during the play, the characters in *Two Trains Running* represent private lives away from the public spotlight whose limited prospects are as much a part of the African American experience as the impassioned oratory and defiant slogans the history of that era celebrates.

Daniel M. Johnson and Rex R. Campbell in their book *Black Migration in America* suggest that the economic upheaval in urban areas during the 1960s and the subsequent loss of employment experienced by urban residents were inevitable for many of those who came from the South to find a better life in the North: "in 1960 only a third (34 percent) of the nation's blacks lived in the North, compared to about 39 percent in 1969."[1] Such metropolitan areas were marked by a decline in wealth because both the industry located in urban areas and the whites who lived there relocated to the suburbs, leaving poor urban blacks to fend for themselves any way they could. Johnson and Campbell explain that "the central cities simultaneously lost some of their aggregate wealth and markedly increased their nonwhite populations, which resulted in greater education, welfare, and transportation needs, while the tax bases declined."[2] Thus, as the tax base declined so did the standard of living and social services in these metropolitan areas. Moreover, the sociological and economic gap in the North increased between "the haves and the have nots," between whites and blacks. These, among others, are the external forces at work in the lives of the characters in *Two Trains Running.*

But there is another key factor that illuminates the psychological impact of this economic decimation. James H. Cone in *Martin & Malcolm & America* expounds upon a precipitous factor perplexing urban blacks originally from the South about their disfranchisement in the North:

> The contrast between what blacks expected to find in the "promised land" of the North and what they actually found there was so great that frustration and despair ensued, destroying much of their self-esteem and dignity. Blacks expected to find the *freedom* which had eluded them for so many years in the South; that is, they expected to have— like other Americans—the right to live wherever they chose and to work and play with whomever they chose. Instead they found themselves crammed into small ghetto sections of the cities, paying to white landlords and merchants exorbitant prices for rent, food, and clothing, and being policed by white cops who showed no more respect for black life than the "white law" they knew so well in the South.[3]

This conflict and contradiction fuels the internal force at work in the hearts and souls of Wilson's characters.

In 1969 Memphis Lee's neighborhood in the city of Pittsburgh is about to become a casualty of progress. Memphis Lee, whose hard work cost him his wife, considers his restaurant "a way to live the rest of my life."[4] Although his restaurant was once a necessary commodity, a thriving business within the community, it is now barely profitable. Originally purchased at $5,500, Memphis's establishment is scheduled for demolition along with nearly a dozen surrounding city blocks. As the play begins, Memphis wants $25,000 from the city to compensate him for the loss of his livelihood. No amount of money can really compensate him for the sense of his place during its heyday, as well as his sense of place within the community: "At one time you couldn't get a seat in here" (9). Currently Memphis's neighborhood is a virtual ghost town: the doctor, the dentist, the supermarket, the five and ten, the staples of any community, are gone.

Wilson derives the action of the play from Memphis and the few patrons who are often embroiled in discussions about themselves and others from their past and present, both living and deceased. It appears that Memphis Lee's restaurant is the only refuge left for the characters in Wilson's play to lift their impoverished spirits and bond together as an extended family. Through their conversations these characters establish a kinship, a community within the safe confines of the restaurant, away from all the violence that occurs outside. Among the living is Wolf, an amicable trickster, sent to jail once essentially for being in the wrong place at the right time, proof that white justice is at best capricious when dealing with the African American. Wolf profits from running numbers for Old Man Albert. Among the dead is the Prophet Samuel, who profited from saving souls and whose wake becomes an event as the play opens, as a long procession of gaping onlookers and mourners winds all the way to West's funeral home. Standing between the living and the dead is West, the wealthy local undertaker, a former gambler and bootlegger, who continually profits from death as Memphis ruefully exclaims, "Ain't nothing going be left but these niggers killing one another . . . West gonna get richer and everybody else gonna get poorer" (9).

Then there are two characters who seem to function as different components in a Greek chorus, Holloway and Hambone. In Greek drama the chorus provides an exposition of past events, a sense of the historical present, or a moral interpretation of the play's events. In *Two Trains Running* the words and views of Holloway and Hambone punctuate the action of the play. They illuminate the predicament of African Americans throughout American history, recalling various injustices of the past and extolling the virtues of those who aid their own in the present.

The character of Hambone recalls the *kommos* by providing a pathetic, cryptic lamentation of black rage against white injustice. In classical Greek drama the *kommos* is a type of lyric, often in dialogue, sung by the chorus to express profound emotion. The aptly named, though seemingly inarticulate, Hambone utters two lines, and throughout the play, often regardless of context, Hambone repeats his mantra: "I want my ham. He gonna give me my ham." The "he" in the second line refers to Lutz, a character physically absent in the play who embodies the deceit of white society. Prior to the play's action, and depending on whose version of the story is believed, Lutz promised Hambone a chicken if he painted his fence, a ham if he painted it well. After Hambone finished the job, though, Lutz gave him only a chicken for a job well done. Hambone wants his ham, not a chicken.

## *TWO TRAINS RUNNING*

This is not the first conversation between Hambone and Lutz, but one that has taken place repeatedly over the course of nine and a half years. Holloway reports that the exchange between the two has left the issue of the ham unresolved and adds that Hambone will not sacrifice his pride or his conviction to set things right, "Cause he ain't willing to accept whatever the white man throw him" (30). Memphis, on the other hand, sarcastically retorts that Hambone's behavior reflects "that old backward Southern mentality," a sense of complacency, that is sadly misplaced in the North (30). Even Hambone's name suggests his predicament. Etymologist Clarence Major provides a clue to Hambone's identity in the following explication of the origin of his name: "in Christianity, Noah considered Ham to be the ancient ancestor of black people," and from the late nineteenth century on, the word *hambone* became a multipurpose metaphor for the "rhythm" of the black cultural experience in music and in life, particularly during the "hard times."[5] Hambone then personifies "hard times" in both his name and his painful, cryptic lamentation, telling of the consequence of a black man's encounter with a white man.

Holloway, in turn, functions as the *stasimon,* commenting upon various topics and providing an oral record of past events. The word *stasimon* in Greek means "stationary song," which the chorus sings, alternating with dialogue delivered by the other characters. Frequently during the play Holloway provides philosophical commentary that places the play's events into a larger context. In one instance, when Memphis claims that black men like Wolf and Sterling are lazy, Holloway puts forth his theory of exponential capitalism, or "stacking," in which white society has always profited from the hard work of African Americans.

The word *stacking* illustrates the inhumane treatment of the African slaves being transported to America during the Middle Passage in intolerably cramped quarters aboard slave ships. Holloway challenges the stereotype that African Americans' poor economic lot in life reflects a shiftless and lazy nature: "People kill me talking about that niggers is lazy. Niggers is the most hard-working people in the world. Worked three hundred years for free. . . . If it wasn't for you the white man would be poor" (34). In the name of progress the African American helped build America, but the problem now facing white society is that it must pay the African American. Holloway ascertains that this change has reduced the African American to an unwanted member of society: "Now that they got to pay you they can't find you none" (35). In the past this peonage system enabled whites to use African Americans to pick their cotton, harvest their crops, and build their railroads and highways. Despite emancipation a pronounced economic chasm remains between blacks and whites in America's capitalistic system—the African Americans who helped build America became the disfranchised because white America's economic progress continued systematically to exclude and thus depreciate the value of the black man.

Mark William Rocha believes that Holloway functions both as "the community elder and oral historian."[6] Rocha states that when director Lloyd Richards stages the play, he positions Holloway in a booth close to the audience so the character can address the predominately white audience. Richards positions this character on the stage in this manner so that Holloway can apprise the audience of an African American's perspective of American history without assuming a prosecutorial pose, which would, in all likelihood, antagonize the audience: "The blocking of the stage action makes explicit the usually implicit theatrical premise that there are two addressees of Holloway's speeches, the other black characters in Memphis's restaurant and the mostly white audiences of Wilson's play. This establishes the triadic relationship that is essential to what in the black vernacular is referred to as 'loud talking.'"[7] Therefore, Rocha proposes that through stagecraft Richards ingeniously disarms the white audience and thus ensures its reception of a black perspective. Rocha suggests that the "loud talking," engendered in the linguistic heritage of African Americans, a manifestation of the African deity Esu, is echoed in the character of Holloway and that "Wilson's play 'tricks' members of the audience into demonstrating their ignorance of the African sensibility [or *'refusal of history'*] that produced the play and shaped the basic assumptions of black culture."[8]

Henry Louis Gates, Jr., explains Esu's linguistic manifestation in the African American vernacular and in doing so sheds light upon how Richards's staging and Wilson's creation of Holloway enable a white audience to experience the history of African Americans: "Esu endlessly displaces meaning, deferring it by the play of signification. . . . He is 'a deceiving shadow,' true to the trickster, "which falls between intent and meaning, between utterance and misunderstanding."[9] In African mythology, specifically Yoruba mythology, Esu is often described as the trickster, often depicted with two mouths, similar to the god Janus is portrayed in Roman mythology. To the Ashanti, this trickster is known as Ananse and as Elegbara to the Fon. Esu's two mouths represent a plurality of thinking, dissenting voices disclosing contradictions, a dialectic, similar to how Rocha describes the function of Holloway's "loud talking," which draws the audience's attention to African American's version of history.

Within this community Aunt Ester represents the oracle that the characters must consult, make offerings to, and entrust their fate to. However, Aunt Ester can also be understood as a female version of the African griot. Although Sandra G. Shannon sees Holloway as "a modernized version of the African griot" providing for the audience the histories of the other characters in the play, Wilson's character of Aunt Ester possesses many of the African griot's attributes.[10] In Africa, the griot is the tribe's historian, one who chronicles history and imparts wisdom within the parameters of an oral tradition and often communicates them in song and rhyme. Aunt Ester always conveys her wisdom through the use of metaphor. Traditionally the great, older male who held a high position within the tribe was a doctor of knowledge and the teller of history. In the African American community the griot may be an elder woman who holds the same esteemed position, much as Aunt Ester does.

All of the characters visit Aunt Ester, seeking her advice and directing their lives according to her pronouncements. The grieving West asks whether his deceased wife is in heaven, and Holloway wants to kill his cursed, servile grandfather, who conceives of God as the white master of heaven, a great plantation where he can eternally pick cotton. Although Aunt Ester does require some money, she refuses to take it, yet still wants for nothing. Wilson explains that in "*Two Trains Running,* there are so many references to death. The undertaker in the black community is the richest man. It's still true today. In the midst of all that, though, in the midst of all this death, you have that which doesn't die—the character of Aunt Ester, which is the tradition."[11] In the play Aunt Ester, a caring yet enigmatic and reclusive matriarch in this African American community, is the antithesis of Prophet Samuel, a man bedecked in jewels even in his casket whose ardent followers are often described more as a harem than a congregation. Despite the contrast between Aunt Ester and Prophet Samuel, also an influential figure within this community, even Prophet Samuel goes to see Aunt Ester.

Prophet Samuel, the former Reverend Samuel, used to broadcast his message through a loudspeaker on a truck throughout the neighborhood. He was arrested for venturing into white neighborhoods where some accused him of hauling away their furniture, and he was eventually charged with income tax evasion due to the wealth of his church. Once he sought Aunt Ester's help, the Reverend Samuel's luck changed: he became Prophet Samuel; the charges against him were dropped; a sizable donation to his church was made; and he began to receive preferential treatment from the mayor and the city police. Upon hearing this story, Sterling decides to seek out Aunt Ester, whose advice convinces him to make a better life for himself and Risa. Following the advice of Aunt Ester is only one means by which many in this community strive to eradicate the stigma of becoming just another symptomatic casualty.

*Two Trains Running* revolves around the theme of money, capitalism, and the connection among hard work, rightful compensation, fate, luck, and identity. Like many people living in poor economic conditions, failing to find legitimate means of support, Wolf and Sterling pursue illegal or suspicious means of income—outside the traditional bounds of accepted occupations. They are part of capitalism's underclass, forced into its underworld. These characters also tend to look for supernatural influences to give them a leg up and provide them with the wealth that will turn their lives around. Wolf and Sterling spend what few dollars they have playing the numbers, relying upon dream books (numerology) to interpret their dreams, seeking the advice of Aunt Ester about their fate, and throwing twenty dollars into the river as an offering to the old sage. At times Holloway employs folk explanations of luck and fate to identify the cause of these characters' sense of displacement and injustice, which in turn then leads to a faith in supernatural intervention: "That's what's wrong with half these niggers now. They don't know what causes their trouble. They around here breaking mirrors, opening umbrellas in the house, and everything else" (90).

Other characters, working within society's legal bounds, demand that their efforts be fairly compensated in real wealth and assert that they have a right to expect economic rewards for their hard work. Memphis, West, and Hambone expect to be remunerated for work they have done. Of course, Wilson does not draw a simple line discretely distinguishing these two types of characters: Sterling works and looks for various jobs in the neighborhood while Wolf has a clear sense of ethics to go along with his strong sense of self-preservation. *Two Trains Running,* then, presents characters who know that there are rewards out there for them; some of the characters have a clear understanding about the means of achieving those rewards while others struggle along hoping that their number will come up one day.

Among the characters who put their faith in hard work and its rewards, Memphis wants the fair-market value for his restaurant, which he must sell to the city as part of its urban renewal campaign. Memphis has placed over thirty years of hard work into his restaurant, losing his wife in the process, and he demands recompense. When West offers him a deal that will compensate him with $15,000 now and another $5,000 later, Memphis knows that West plans to use his property along with West's own property to negotiate a healthy settlement from the city. Memphis understands enough of the capitalist system not to let West tease him with short-term money and thereby lose out on the long-term rewards West knows are out there. Memphis even holds out when the court offers him $20,000 for his property, stridently claiming that he wants $30,000 and not a penny less.

Wilson uses Memphis's obstinate attitude to create tension in the play much in the way he uses Troy Maxson's assertiveness on the job in *Fences*. Troy goes to the union and insists that the door to a better job be opened to him, and he holds his ground and receives the promotion he deserves. But the audience, like Rose and Bono, does not know what the future holds for Troy. Although the times are changing, the audience does not know if they are changing enough to accommodate this one character's demands. So too the audience senses that Memphis may wind up with nothing if the city asserts its right of eminent domain and lays claim to his property, much in the way Stoval seized Memphis's property in Mississippi years earlier. Yet Memphis works the system to his own advantage, hiring a white attorney to plead his case before the court and receiving $35,000 for his property in the play's conclusion.

West is another character whose hard work and capitalistic confidence garner him financial rewards, although West's livelihood is dependent exclusively on the African American community, not the larger white society. In a community marked by economic decline, as Daniel R. Fusfeld and Timothy Bates assert, "the state of the ghetto business community reflects the economic circumstances of its clientele," which certainly explains West's choice of occupation.[12] West's field of business, although not his first choice, to be a rancher and horse breeder like his grandfather, relates to his philosophical credo, which acerbically recalls Booker T. Washington's views of gradual economic advantage leading to gradual social equality.

When West encourages Sterling to be patient and realistic in realizing his dreams of obtaining money and a good woman, advising Sterling to "Carry you a little cup and you'll never be disappointed," he reiterates the rhetoric of Booker T. Washington. West claims that in order to be content in life Sterling should carry "a little cup" so that it seems like something when it fills up. In contrast, Sterling possesses a get-rich-quick or carpe-diem philosophy, which West refers to as Sterling's "ten-gallon bucket [that] ain't never gonna be full" (94). In this analogy to a bucket West slights the allegorical paradigm of the bucket that Booker T. Washington in his "The Atlanta Exposition Address" claimed all African Americans should "cast down." This speech, also known as "The Atlanta Compromise," reveals Washington's nonmilitant posture to race relations, especially between the sons and daughters of former slave owners in the South and the sons and daughters of former slaves.

## *TWO TRAINS RUNNING*

Washington envisioned this position as a means for black Americans as citizens to secure the right to, at least, a low-level economic opportunity within America's industrial age. Washington repeats the phrase "cast down your bucket where you are"—initially as a call for reconciliation between the races but then as an invitation to both blacks and whites to negotiate and invest themselves in a mutually beneficial economic partnership: "No race can prosper till it learns that there is as much dignity in tilling a field as in writing a poem. It is at the bottom of life we must begin, and not at the top. Nor should we permit our grievances to overshadow our opportunities."[13] West's advice to Sterling resembles Holloway's discussion with Memphis regarding Sterling's prospects for landing steady employment. Memphis argues that a few dollars earned from many hours of legitimate work is better than the alternative of no money at all. Holloway responds that the ten dollars a young man like Sterling earns today will be spent quickly on necessities, leaving him nothing left to show for all his hard work. Holloway also employs the analogy of a bucket. Unlike Washington's bucket, which promises advancement and acceptance every time it is hauled up, this bucket has a hole in the bottom, which keeps the African American working harder while making no progress: "Like trying to haul sand in a bucket with a hole in it. Time you get where you going the bucket empty. That's why that ten dollar a day ain't gonna do him no good" (34).

West as a businessman expects to make a reasonable profit from caskets and funerals. When Risa wants Hambone to be buried in a bronze casket even though the state only compensates West for the cost of a pine one, he holds his ground with Risa, refusing to be manipulated by pity or guilt to lose money. He has already decided to lay out Hambone for free, since the welfare money does not cover this, and he believes that any further concessions on his part represent foolish business practices. When Risa dreams of having the money for a bronze or gold casket that will prove Hambone's life was worth something, West confidently employs the discourse of commerce and capitalism: "I don't get them for free, woman. I call the company and order the casket, they send me the bill. . . . People don't understand. I got overhead. I got seven cars I got to keep up. Got supplies I got to order. How much you think that embalming fluid cost. I got all kinds of bills. People owe me money and won't pay me. It ain't all like everybody think with Mr. West" (92).

It is easy to hear West's words as heartless expressions of materialism, but Hambone himself understood quite well West's point. Hambone spent the last nine and a half years of his life trying to collect wages due him from Lutz. After walking over to the fence that Hambone painted for Lutz, Sterling recognizes the hard work Hambone put into the job. Sterling notes that even after all these years of wear the quality of Hambone's work is evident. After contemplating buying Hambone his coveted ham, Sterling realizes that what appears to be madness in Hambone is actually his focus for living: "I started to go over there and get his ham for him. But then he wouldn't have nothing to do in the morning. I didn't want to take that away from him. He have more cause to get up out of bed in the morning than I do. I consider him lucky" (50). Hambone has chosen to stand up for his material rights. The fact that he takes his quest for compensation so far that it consumes his consciousness appears superficially like madness, but Hambone has more in common with Memphis than Memphis would like to believe.

Although Memphis treats Hambone rather roughly throughout the play, denying him even a cup of free coffee, his line "but my clause say . . . they got to meet my price" expresses the ethos of Hambone's "He gonna give me my ham. I want my ham" (60). Like Hambone, Memphis has been denied what was his by right. Both have been exploited by whites who used either their own standards or legal subtleties to justify their actions. Hambone's history is muted. Though the few words he utters in the course of the play refer to one event in his life, the scars that cover his body silently recall a long history of suffering, of which the last nine and half years are only one part.

Memphis also has a history that he keeps alive, waiting for the day when he can set it right. Some day Memphis plans to return, drive a V-8 Ford past Stoval's house, and wave to the house's inhabitant. Later he will return, not with a wave, but with a 30.06 hunting rifle. Memphis conceives of time primarily in terms of past and future in contrast to Hambone who conceives of time in terms of a continuous present. To Memphis it is only a matter of time till the city officials, through negotiations with his white lawyer Joseph Bartoromo, give him his $25,000, which will compensate Memphis and prepare him to seek restitution for the past. That moment in Memphis's future stands in opposition to the moment in the past when Memphis failed to receive just payment from Stoval. These two moments, one past and one future, dominate Memphis's thinking throughout the play.

## UNDERSTANDING AUGUST WILSON

Hambone, in contrast, lives in a perpetually present moment of anticipation where the passage of nine and a half years—such a long time to the other characters—is focused exclusively on his rightful payment. Many critics have described Hambone as mentally retarded or deficient in some way, but Wilson's stage directions do not suggest that Hambone is mentally retarded, only consumed by his desire for just compensation: "*[Hambone] is self-contained and in a world of his own. His mental condition has deteriorated to such a point that he can only say two phrases . . .*" (14).

While Hambone over the years has proclaimed the violation he has suffered at the hands of Lutz, Memphis has developed a corresponding attitude over time: "Once I know the rules, whatever they are, I can play by them" (73). West has learned the same lesson. But there is a price to be paid. In 1931 Stoval used a legal stipulation to take possession of Memphis's land. To ensure his power over Memphis, Stoval kills Memphis's mule and burns his crops. When relaying the story to the patrons in his restaurant, Memphis claims that in order to "get to my house I'd have to walk though fire. I wasn't ready to do that" (73). In 1969 the city wants to take Memphis's restaurant for a mere $15,000. Memphis knows that he risks everything by holding out; the restaurant may go up in flames, and he will receive nothing for his property. But time has taught Memphis a lesson that allows him to stand up to the city in a way he could not stand up to Stoval: "See, they don't know. The half ain't never been told. I'm ready to walk through fire. . . . That's the way I feel now. They don't know I got a clause of my own" (59–60). Memphis's success lies in making the law work for him, and he is one of the few characters in August Wilson's play who succeeds financially. He makes the system work for him, much in the way West does.

Then there is Risa Thomas, another character, like Hambone, who has no clear past, only a seemingly endless present as Memphis's less than dynamic waitress. Risa is an attractive, insular young woman, one character who is especially compassionate toward Hambone. A member of Prophet Samuel's First African Congressional Kingdom, Risa mutilated herself by slashing her legs to ward off the attention of men like Sterling whom she believes have nothing but lascivious intentions toward her. Sandra G. Shannon in "The Ground on Which I Stand" interprets the waitress in Memphis's diner as yet another example of a black woman in the role of nurturer. It is from this perspective of Risa as nurturer that Shannon explores the delicate relationship between Risa and Hambone and points to the "physical and emotional scars that seem to forge a common bond between them."[14] Aside from the connection between Risa's self-inflicted cuts and the multiple scars on Hambone's body, Shannon suggests that the emotional connection between the two is a sign of the emotional scars that unite them psychologically. The recipients of Risa's form of domestic nurturing are not actual family members in this setting but surrogates; the restaurant functions as a home, and its patrons, with the exception of Sterling, act as grandfathers, fathers, uncles, and brothers.

Wilson stated in an interview that the image of "two trains running" is a metaphor that foreshadows the play's theme. Because the title came before the inception of the play's characters, it becomes an image that conveys implicitly the possible personal and sociological reasons for Memphis's anger:

There were two ideas in the play, or at least two ideas that have confronted black America since the Emancipation, the ideas of cultural assimilation and cultural separatism. These were in my mind the two trains running. I wanted to write a play about a character for whom neither of these trains were working. He had to build a new railroad in order to get where he was going, because the trains are not going his way. That was the idea when I started out exploring.[15]

In an interview with Lloyd Richards—Wilson's longtime friend, mentor, and collaborator—Richard Pettengill asked the director to comment on this play in relation to the others:

August has done here what he has done in all the plays he has written. His plays have centered themselves in the decade and have illuminated the life of an oppressed people during that time. He has not approached the plays as historical chronologies of the events of the time, or even as dialogues on the problems of a time. He has approached everything through characters, characters who any of us may have encountered or avoided encountering on the street. He has put them in a position where we can get to know them through their attempts to deal with the issues of their time as they affect their everyday lives. And in their struggle to live, to survive, to thrive, one begins to perceive these people in their time; you see the history flowing to the time and flowing from it as it affects the lives and decisions of those characters.[16]

## *TWO TRAINS RUNNING*

As Richards implies, in *Two Trains Running* Wilson chronicles the post–Civil Rights era, not on the grand scheme as a documentarian would, but on an intimate level through the scope and dimension of his characters. Thus, a discussion regarding the African American's historical relationship to the white society's capitalistic endeavors leads the patrons of Memphis's restaurant into another topic relevant to the post–Civil Rights era, politics. When Sterling invites Risa to a rally to celebrate Malcolm X's birthday, before she can reply, Memphis and Holloway respond. Memphis emphasizes that it was blacks who killed Malcolm, implying that such a celebration is just political hypocrisy. Holloway says that he would choose Aunt Ester, the living community griot, to celebrate instead.

To Holloway the aged, modest Aunt Ester is the oracle who epitomizes the longevity of wisdom and the vernacular, for she speaks in a language native to the African American community. While she represents a virtual continuum, a sense of communal history, Aunt Ester is a local figure, not one lauded nationally as a messiah commanding disciples. Holloway contends that Malcolm's greatness and popularity destined him for the tragic fate of saints, martyrdom: "Malcolm got too big. People call him a saint. That's what the problem was. He got too big, and when you get that big ain't nothing else you could do. . . . When you get to be a saint there ain't nothing else for you can do but die. The people wouldn't have it any other way" (41). Memphis then metaphorically compares the fates of Malcolm X and Martin Luther King, Jr.: "If they kill the sheep you know what they do to the wolf" (41). Memphis is too cynical to believe that celebrating fallen leaders will result in any serious improvement in anyone's lot, as the current unrest in his neighborhood indicates: "Ain't nothing gonna be left but these niggers killing one another . . ." (9).

With these leaders gone, it is left to individuals to come to grips with injustices past and present, north and south. Therefore, it seems telling that both Memphis Lee and Hambone experience ubiquitous forms of economic and racial injustice— Memphis down south in Mississippi and Hambone up north in Pittsburgh. Not unlike other older generations of African Americans, Memphis saw firsthand the surmounting pressures upon the Civil Rights Movement, the divisions within the movement, and its slow progress on the road to equity. Memphis proclaims that slogans such as "black is beautiful" and notions of real black power will not rectify this dire situation of spiritual or economic impoverishment. At times violence is the only answer to white injustice: "Talking about black power with their hands and their pockets empty. You can't do nothing without a gun. That's the only power the white man understand" (42).

Sterling wants to attend the Malcolm X rally to demonstrate black power or solidarity, not to look for messiahs who promise to deliver them from socio-economic misery. Later in the play, when Memphis sees a rally flyer on the wall of his establishment placed there by Sterling, he reiterates his point and cites the ineffectual outcome of a rally that lasted three weeks over the case of the defenseless Begaboo boy who was shot by the police: "All them niggers wanna do is have a rally. Soon as they finish with one rally, they start planning the next. They forget what goes on in between. You rally to spur you into action. When it comes times for action these niggers sit down and scratch their heads . . ." (85). James H. Cone argues that "It is not easy to survive in a society that says you do not count. Many do not survive. With the absence of black pride, that 'I am somebody' feeling, many young African Americans have no respect for themselves or anybody else. . . . If something radical is not done soon to put an end to this madness, the African American community will soon commit suicide against itself."[17] Action, sometimes, means guns in the hands of the black man. Holloway says that a gun in the hands of a black man only signals trouble and arrest by the white man; Memphis cynically claims that the gun just means another funeral, another job for West.

Although it is Sterling who expresses the need for black power, perhaps initially as a means to secure a date to the rally with Risa, Sterling seems to understand Memphis's point about the power of violence. On his own since the age of eighteen, and before that shuttled off unwanted to an orphanage, Sterling robbed a bank because he "was tired of waking up every day with no money," so he went where white men like Mellon had theirs (45–46). Sterling says about life, "I was sorry that I was ever born into it" (52). From Sterling's comment, the audience would assume he is a fatalist, yet he has the passion of a survivor.

Sterling, an ex-con, thinks himself lucky, comparing himself to the great prizefighter Joe Louis. Sterling is always looking for capital, as evidenced when he first enters Memphis's diner and tries to sell his watch to one of the patrons. He tries to sell Memphis five gallons of gas from a can he found in the alley, attempts to secure employment from West by driving the black funeral Cadillacs, and considers selling chicken sandwiches at the local steel mill during lunchtime—all while courting Risa and promising her a better life. However, Sterling's involvement with the gas can he claims to have found remains suspect, particularly when the drugstore down the street burns down one night. Popular rhetoric, those rallying cries of black power, seem to be mere political gestures to Sterling. In Sterling's personal life he thrives upon dreams of winning at craps in Vegas, the companionship of a good woman, and a Cadillac or two. He thinks playing the numbers might be the solution; the underside of capitalism has worked for Wolf, even Memphis and West, the two most economically secure people in the play. Finally, Sterling does select the right numbers, numbers which reflect the self-inflicted scars on each of Risa's legs.

In *Two Trains Running* Wilson exposes his predominately white audience to the richness of the black vernacular; his play is "permeated with such displays of signifyin(g)" as "sounding," Wolf's verbal assaults; as "rapping," Sterling's verbal foreplay with Risa, a sign of one's verbal dexterity; as "marking," Holloway's mimicking the verbal nuances of another's speech when telling a story; and as "loudtalking," Hambone's verbal accusations meant specifically to shame Lutz but generally to decry white injustice.[18] Wilson also uses storytelling as an essential narrative device in the play—an invitation extended to the audience to enter the black community and witness both orally and visually that community. In one instance Sterling asks Hambone to repeat the phrases "Black is beautiful," "United we stand; Divided we fall" and "Malcolm lives" as a rallying cry amongst "Brothers" (63–65). To his pleasure, Hambone mimics him. Yet when Sterling disrupts this cry with Hambone's complaint, "I want my ham," Hambone can no longer be encum-

*TWO TRAINS RUNNING*

bered by Sterling's rhetoric, for it is artificial, not psychologically synchronistic to Hambone's qualified sense of time, purpose, or personal story.

At the end of the play one event occurring offstage, Hambone's death, shifts the focus. Although Hambone's body surrenders, tires from Lutz's injustice, his spirit survives. Hambone's death effects an essential change in the characters of Sterling, Risa, and Memphis. Sterling and Risa begin a genuine relationship, and Memphis's property settlement with the city is resolved for more money than he expected. Prophetically, Aunt Ester advises Memphis "to go back and pick up the ball," to travel back to Jackson and settle his dispute with Stovall (109). Realizing that Hambone never dropped the ball, as a tribute Memphis asks Risa to buy some flowers for the funeral and to sign the card from "everybody who ever dropped the ball and went to pick it up" (110). Although Hambone never dropped the ball, he did lose all his history except for his deal with Lutz, as West reveals: "Hambone ain't had no people. Most anybody know about him is he come from Alabama. Don't even know his right name" (90).

Ultimately it is Hambone's death that in some small way provides these characters with a means of salvation, a preservation of their dignity, and a deliverance from the misfortune that has befallen each of them. At the end of the play Hambone is posthumously liberated from the injustice of the white man. Sterling breaks into Lutz's store and steals a ham, which is placed alongside Hambone in his casket. West as the funeral director complies, for he is used to placing Bibles, canes, crutches, guitars, radios, baby dolls, and even tomatoes in with the deceased.

Though West says, "Dead folks don't know nothing," these personal relics are important for the living to venerate their dead and for the dead to have something of value for all time (37).

# CHAPTER SEVEN

# *Seven Guitars*

As *Seven Guitars* begins, five friends gather together in the backyard of a house in Pittsburgh to reminisce about the life of their absent friend, a local blues guitarist named Floyd Barton, whose sudden death elicits in them the impetus to reexamine their lives in relation to his. The year is 1948. Attired in their Sunday best, Canewell, Vera, Louise, Red, and Hedley have just returned from the cemetery where their deceased friend, one in the usual group of seven, Floyd "Schoolboy" Barton, has been laid to rest. As a befitting tribute to the life of a musician, the landlady Louise breaks out in song. She sings a bawdy, slightly irreverent, song which quickly transforms what could be a mournful occasion into one more jovial. With food and drink at hand, the mourners begin to share stories about Floyd and gradually reveal their personal lives.

Death and all it entails is a topic of discussion. Vera and Canewell attest to seeing angels at the cemetery who were looking for Floyd. Upon hearing these testimonials, Red Carter admits that he sees one, and Louise remains skeptical in the presence of the others. Vera insists that they were six in number, equal in number to the mourners, and that they transported the soul of Floyd upward, toward the direction of heaven, an observation that surprises Red Carter, who had assumed that Floyd's eternal destination would be hell.

Akin to the Greeks' concept of *moira,* or fate, the angels represent the parts his friends played in Floyd's brief life, the parts the characters assume in their own lives, and, as the play unfolds, the ultimate role Floyd plays in the other characters' lives. These characters' destinies are intertwined. Throughout most of the play Wilson reveals the synergistic relationship Floyd has to the other characters in the form of a retrospective structure, a series of flashbacks to a few days before his death. The retrospective unites the remaining six characters, including Louise's niece Ruby, who later appears in act 1, through their personal histories. Hence, the title *Seven Guitars* evokes the image of the players, the characters, as separate but at times convergent members in the creation of a shared, polyphonic history. So together they continue to celebrate the life of Floyd as each hears the recording of Floyd Barton singing "That's All Right," a song which permeates this elegiac atmosphere as well as each character's consciousness.

Wilson's choice of song is not incidental when the reader compares the life of its originator to the life of the fictional Floyd "Schoolboy" Barton. Barton's recording, which is played as a tribute, is a rendition of Arthur Crudrup's number titled "That's All Right," echoing a line from Blind Lemon Jefferson's blues song "That Black Snake Moon." Crudrup, a blues guitarist and vocalist from rural Mississippi, traveled to Chicago like his fictional counterpart to record his work. Crudrup recorded that blues number in Chicago in 1946 on the Bluebird label, RCA Victor's label for black musicians, a similar event within a time-frame attributed to the fictional Floyd "Schoolboy" Barton in Wilson's play. And just like the real Crudrup, Barton too never earned his money in royalties, as his friends affirm.

## *SEVEN GUITARS*

Wilson transports the audience a few days back in time to provide a glimpse into the characters' individual and collective pasts. The playwright begins by furnishing the audience with a retrospective view of Floyd and Vera's passionate, yet troubled relationship. In the same backyard, a thirty-five-year-old Floyd is seen playfully seducing, with all the charm he can muster, a rightfully suspicious Vera, eight years younger than he, to accompany him to Chicago. Floyd on one of his many excursions to Chicago had fallen prey to another woman, Pearl Brown, and is trying to make amends with Vera. Anticipating rejection, Floyd sent a love letter to Vera that he had someone else compose. Since "some fellow down in the workhouse be writing everybody letters," the ingenious Floyd had him write one to Vera for 50 cents.[1]

This letter and other documents illustrate that Floyd believes in the power of written discourse, to use his word, "papers," to enhance his oral discourse. Floyd makes this point to Canewell, referring to one particular "paper" that documents the pay he should receive during the days of his incarceration at the workhouse: "That's supposed to give you a starting place" (33). Papers such as the love letter to Vera, the letter from Savoy Records, the letter from the workhouse, and the pawn shop receipt for his electric guitar enable Floyd to seize the opportunity to validate his identity as a man, as a musician, and as an African American male in the 1940s. A problem with the latter two documents arises; he has only the envelope that contained those papers from the workhouse, and the pawn shop receipt is expired. All Floyd wants is a starting place: some money of his own, some opportunity to play his music, and someone to love. As the *New Yorker* theater critic John Lahr observes, "Opportunity is what Floyd carries in his pocket when he is conjured up before us in his high-stepping, smooth-talking glory."[2]

Floyd gingerly reinvents himself as a victim of circumstance. An inventive storyteller, Floyd elaborates to Vera that he and this fellow Canewell were inmates at the workhouse because he was arrested for vagrancy, or, as he says, "worthlessness," in Chicago. But when Vera interrupts his story and says that she heard a different version from Canewell, that Floyd threatened to burn down the jailhouse, he quickly re-constructs his version of events and attributes his lengthy sentence to a misunderstanding. Actually this misunderstanding occurred when his words were misinterpreted by a smug white guard as a threat to burn the jailhouse down, and the judge sentenced him unfairly to ninety days.

Canewell too was arrested in Chicago on numerous charges: disturbing the peace, loitering, resisting arrest, and soliciting without a license. While he was waiting for Floyd, Canewell decided to set down his hat and play his harmonica, and he was sentenced to thirty days: "They rolled all that together and charged me with laziness and give me thirty days" (23). Both men envision their arrests in terms of absurd, yet profoundly held, ethnocentric stereotypes: worthlessness and laziness. Floyd believes that a black man can be arrested anywhere and relates the story of when he was arrested for loitering in Pittsburgh on the day he buried his mother.

Unfairness is expected when these characters confront a legal system constructed and enforced by whites, "cause he know the black man ain't never had his druthers" (41–42). That is, the word *druthers* represents no options for the black man except to submit. As they begin to exchange their stories of wrongful incarceration, Red claims that he was once arrested for possessing too much money because the officer just assumed that he had committed a robbery.

Floyd presents a solution to righting those wrongs against black men with his .38, and the others begin to expound upon their choice of weapons like those who relish in displaying their battle scars, the bigger the better. Floyd carries a .38 Smith and Wesson; Red carries a snubnose .32 pistol; Canewell carries a "professional" pocket knife; and Hedley brandishes an immense butcher's knife, his chicken knife. These black men feel they need to protect themselves, their rights as citizens, in an America that many black men fought for during World War II. Floyd shows his patriotism when he states to Canewell that America won the war and ridicules their choice of weapons as inferior; knives for him are anachronistic weapons in an era where fire power is vital, in the age of the atomic bomb. From a political standpoint Wilson's comments to Lahr pertaining to African American history after the war clarify Floyd's point further: "We had gone off and demonstrated our allegiance and willingness to die for the country. We actually believed that things would be different, and that we would be accorded first-class citizenship. We came back after the war, and that was not true."[3]

Things were not different, though. Floyd's past confrontations with the white man reveal this inequity for the black man in America. Floyd produces a letter from Savoy Records to impress Vera, evidence that he has the opportunity to showcase his talent in a Chicago recording studio, and then a connection to Floyd's cunning manager, T. L. Hall is made. Floyd knows that he must negotiate within the white community in order to salvage his dreams of recording his music.

The dialogue between the two characters exposes Vera's vulnerability. Essentially her sense of self-worth is contingent upon her ability to satisfy Floyd. Floyd's affair with Pearl Brown proves to Vera that what she had to offer was not enough. Vera poignantly and sensuously describes her loneliness after Floyd had left: "After I had walked through an empty house for a year and a half looking for you. After I lay myself out on that bed and search my body for your fingerprints. 'He touched me here . . . and he kissed me here and . . . he ain't here he ain't here quit looking for him cause he ain't here he's there!'" (14). Vera's heartfelt words are sufficient to instill guilt in Floyd and leave the issue of her accompanying Floyd to Chicago unresolved through most of the play. The phrase that best describes Vera's problematic relationship with Floyd is what Louise calls "man trouble" (15). Vera, perplexed by her own vacillation, sums up her predicament aptly: "That's what the problem is now. Everybody keep their trunk packed up. Time you put two and two together and try to come up with four . . . they out the door" (28). Like Vera, Louise's twenty-five-year-old niece Ruby has man trouble. Ruby arrives soon due to "man trouble" she had in Alabama.

In Wilson's plays the psychological repercussions of "man trouble" are all too common for many of his female characters; it is a gendered struggle experienced to various degrees. In act 1 Louise and Vera discuss their travails with love. They identify the mementos their men left behind as tangible reminders of their mutual forlorn relationships: Floyd had left an old guitar behind with Vera, and Louise was left with only a razor, shoes, and a pistol from a twelve-year relationship with a man named Henry. Louise, forty-eight and wiser, proposes that if Vera does go to Chicago with Floyd, she should find a faithful man because in all likelihood Floyd will continue to stray.

Wilson has admitted that creating female characters is difficult:

I doubt seriously if I could make a woman the focus of my work simply because of the fact that I am a man, and I guess because of the ground on which I stand and the viewpoint from which I perceive the world. I can't do that although I try to be honest in the instances in which I do have women. I try to portray them from their own viewpoint as opposed to my viewpoint. I try to—to the extent I am able—to step around on the other side of the table, if you will, and try to look at things from their viewpoint and have been satisfied that I have been able to do so to some extent.[4]

Sandra G. Shannon argues that the female characters assume the traditional role of nurturer in Wilson's plays, a role based in part because of their ability to sustain others and in part because men have thrust that role on them. Shannon believes this role has been "sustained," historically inscribed in their psyches "from slavery through the Great Migration to the North."[5] Thus, the real difficulty for Wilson becomes how to go beyond what one might perceive as this "conventional" type of black women on stage in his plays. The only way to confront this prescribed role of nurturer is through dialogue. Shannon asserts that when Wilson creates dialogue for these women to voice their desire "to break free of male definition" as nurturers, he attempts conscientiously to mitigate their subordination to the male characters.[6]

Harry J. Elam, Jr., also examines Wilson's attempt to include the female voice and viewpoint onstage. In "August Wilson's Women," Elam says, "Wilson's black female characters also challenge orthodoxy and press against historical limitations, recognizing and confronting the additional burdens placed upon them by gender. Limited by their subordinate position within the patriarchy, the women in Wilson's dramas attempt to establish relationships with men on their own terms."[7] It becomes a struggle in which Wilson too, as a male playwright, must engage in his creation of female characters.

These psychological repercussions arise when Louise, who is no stranger to "man trouble," acts as nurturer to Hedley and conveys through dialogue what both Shannon and Elam have described as "a woman needing a man."[8] During one of their encounters Hedley sings a refrain of a song similar to one version recorded by Jelly Roll Morton in 1940 titled "Buddy Bolden Blues." This song is about the late Charles "Buddy" Bolden, a legendary cornet player from New Orleans often called the "First Man of Jazz." Bolden's moniker "King" is also the name given to Hedley by his father, an admirer of the musician.[9] Male hegemony is inscribed within this song, and each time Hedley sings the song, the connections among Bolden, Hedley, his father, and, later, Floyd are announced. Louise's discourse is silenced, outside Hedley's distinctly male discourse, the song with its masculine referents. Moreover, when Louise expresses to Hedley that she hopes that Floyd will just pack the belongings that he left behind, excluding Vera's heart, and leave, again male hegemony asserts itself in a connection between the real life musician Buddy Bolden of Hedley's song and Floyd Barton.

Noting the charismatic personality of Bolden, author Harnett T. Kane writes that "Bolden had two loves, music and women. Women fought to hold his coat. He made up songs, his rich voice stirred the girls. His playing had one indispensable feature, "the entrance. . . ."[10] From a feminist standpoint, the same traits ascribed to Bolden are attributed to Floyd, whether he is corporeally present or not, and to the subject of Hedley's song. Black feminist scholar bell hooks criticizes Wilson's *Fences* for his perpetuation of male hegemony in the behavior of Rose: "patriarchy is not critiqued, and even though tragic expressions of conventional masculinity are evoked, sexist values are reinscribed via the black woman's redemption message. . . ."[11] The same could be said of the actions of Vera, Louise, and Ruby in their relationships with men in *Seven Guitars*.

Of course, what is uppermost in Louise's mind is Hedley's health, for he has contracted tuberculosis. Louise demands that Hedley visit the local white doctor named Goldblum and assures him that blacks can enter the sanitariums now. Hedley refuses; he will only trust a member from his community to restore his health after his father had died because of a negligent white doctor. Hedley claims that curative measures such as the natural root tea and powders of the local black healer Miss Sarah Degree, whom he deems a saint, seem to be restoring his health. To

Hedley, any interaction with or connection to whites signifies his subordination as a black man. When Canewell says that he was going to bring his Bible but brought the goldenseal plant, from which Miss Sarah Degree's tea is made, to plant in the yard, Hedley tells a brief story of his grandmother's use of the plant. Folk beliefs, Christianity, and Hedley's blues seep into his discourse: an Afrocentric discussion of the Bible and its contents, a reference to the great Jamaican-born black nationalist Marcus Garvey's statement, "Ethiopia shall spread forth her wings and every abomination shall be brought low," and the story about Hedley's relationship to his father are juxtaposed in an elliptical manner (19).

Hedley's storytelling is magnificent in scope in that he frames these profoundly idiosyncratic stories within a fairy-tale-like structure. Hedley dreams of money that will transform his existence as a marginalized black man, money that will come to him from the legendary Buddy Bolden to buy a plantation. This dream for now is unrealized, and instead of money all that Hedley receives are ashes. Ashes are a symbol of the death of the dream Hedley refuses to relinquish. In history Bolden must repay a loan from Hedley's father, a poor man whose labors for the white man go unrecognized and whose pride must, at all cost, be redeemed in Hedley's mind. This plantation, a symbol of the white man's subjugation of the black man, will allow Hedley to free himself from the yoke of second-class citizen or, in his thinking, obtain his father's forgiveness.

Canewell, a storyteller too, complements Hedley's grand scheme by inquiring what crops Hedley will grow on this vast plantation and in the process reveals the origin of his surname.

His grandfather used to harvest sugarcane in Louisiana, and the only recognition of his labor was the name Canewell, for someone commented about his grandfather, "That boy can cane well" (25). Canewell adds in jest that if he had been born elsewhere his name just as easily could have been "Cottonwell," a comment in which he unknowingly identifies the precarious nomenclature used to describe the African Americans' historical disfranchisement in the South. As writer Jeff Yang affirms, names become "a principal component of our personalities, perhaps even a portion of our souls." Names elicit a point of reference, and "they shackle us to family, ancestry, history."[12] Unfortunately, Yang asserts, names can also "conscribe us, compress our identities into a few rude syllables." Thus, in the origin of Canewell's name, his African American identity is reduced to a white man's linguistic construction, namely "boy" and "cane well"—signifying his subordinate position within the socio-economic structure of American history. Canewell's final words on the subject of his name are illuminating : "Sugar [cane] beat many a man down" (25). Conversely, in Floyd's "signifying," ironic version of Hedley's plantation dream in which Hedley is seated on a porch and drinking mint juleps, the distinction between those who marginalize and those marginalized is blurred, for in this version Hedley assumes the role of the white aristocratic plantation owner.

Most characters in the play assume Hedley's dream reflects his mental instability. Hedley is simply burdened by his past. His father was always the black man, both psychologically and socio-economically, under the "boot" of the white man (67). The kicks that his father administers to him in a dream are the source of Hedley's motivation to be a respected black man: "He comes to me in a dream. He say, 'Are you my son?' I say, 'Yes, Father, I am your son.' He say, 'I kick you in the mouth?' I say, 'Yes, Father, I ask you why you do nothing and you kick me.' He say, 'Do you forgive me,' I say, 'Yes, Father, I forgive you' . . ." (70). The word *Father* is capitalized in the play text to display that Hedley's reverence for his father resembles references to God the "Father" in the Bible. Hedley's father's life, his spirit for survival, thrives within his son's memory. When Hedley digs a hole for Vera to place the goldenseal, the plant represents more than its curative powers. Hedley finds a symbolic place to plant his dream. Just as he warns Vera not to let the roots of the plant dry out, for they dry out easily, Hedley despite his age, ill health, and poverty must constantly nourish his dream through the act of telling it.[13]

In Wilson's play Hedley's creative, yet certainly idiosyncratically structured, storytelling ability surpasses even Floyd's mastery of oral discourse. The final demise of Floyd will rest upon the competition between these two storytellers, as foreshadowed in Floyd's attempt to alter Hedley's narrative about Buddy Bolden. To Floyd's "Wake up and give me the money," Hedley recites the lyrics "'Come here. Here go the money'" (23). Hedley corrects Floyd because he attempts to assume a voice that is not his own. Floyd violates the narrative parameters of Hedley's discourse.

Just as there is a gender-bound community of unrequited women among these seven friends, there is a gender-bound community of men who share some of their personal stories of survival with "woman trouble." The male characters are confounded by women who defy their traditional expectations as nurturers or sexual objects. Red tells the tall tale about a plan he devised to satisfy seven women, one for every day of the week. To his dismay, it was a plan that failed miserably because each woman desired his company on Friday night, payday. Red's tale of woe is due to a woman's greed, or so he claims. To resolve this problem and maintain his sanity, Red quits his job and settles for one woman, WillaMae. Although Red's WillaMae just had a baby boy, Red Carter's desire for other women lends credence to Louise's views of men. Red seems interested only in the prospect of meeting some "pretty women" in the big city (35).

Canewell too, who has eyes for Vera, seems to have "woman trouble." He attempts to advise the other males how to treat a woman tenderly: "You know how to tell if a watermelon is sweet? You don't thump them. You treat a watermelon just like you do a woman . . . you squeeze them" (38). Canewell who used to be with a woman named Lulu Johnson, now resides with an old woman because he refuses to invest himself in a permanent relationship. This wanderlust spirit is also what Vera fears most in her relationship with Floyd, who is seduced by Pearl Brown simply because she believed in him. Oddly, Pearl's emotional support links her to his mother. Floyd's fondness for his mother is clear. When he collects his meager wages from the workhouse, sells an old guitar so that he can buy back his electric guitar, and secures a play date at a local club, Floyd plans to use the remaining money to buy his beloved mother an engraved gravestone.

During a slapstick pepper-eating contest between Hedley and Red, which disrupts their discourse on women, Wilson uses Red's nearly tripping over Floyd's guitar as a segue to a music-as-mistress discussion. Floyd confides to the others that music is an integral part of his life. Canewell feels the same but maintains that he possesses neither the talent nor the ambition that Floyd has. Canewell claims that he heard the calling, like music to his ears, to be a preacher, but jests that the devil spoke louder: "God speak in a whisper and the devil shout" (45). It is then that the audience learns that within the local pawnshop lie Red's drums, Canewell's harmonica, and along side them Floyd's electric guitar.

For the loss of their instruments and obvious lack of funds, the characters naturally blame Floyd's stealthy manager, Mr. T. L. Hall. Floyd explains that he has no control over how the music business operates and is equally a victim of those big-city record producers, which echoes the views of the various band members in *Ma Rainey's Black Bottom*. John Lahr remarks, "For these characters, work is hard-scrabble, but fun isn't. Wilson makes a point of showing off their high spirits and their talent when, after some artful engineering badinage, the band members find themselves making wonderful music out of nothing."[14] Disagreements aside, these men react to one another in waves of musical spontaneity. They all play on some makeshift instruments with the exception of Canewell, who pulls out his harmonica: Red with his drumsticks raps upon the table; Hedley with his homemade one-string instrument, which produces a somewhat melodic note, plucks the string; and Floyd accompanies the rest by strumming upon his old guitar.

Hedley plays his handmade instrument, a one-string device that mentally reconnects him to his past, and recalls how his grandfather's playing upon a similar instrument would elicit memories of his grandfather's late mother's prayers. Floyd remembers his own mother's gentle voice, her prayers, and her encouragement. Missing the sound of her prayers, Floyd begins to sing "The Lord's Prayer" and, after he is finished, promises out loud to purchase a proper marker for her grave, a grave situated in the unkempt, weed-strewn, poor section of the cemetery— the portion of the cemetery designated for blacks.

In both life and death disfranchisement befalls these African Americans as Canewell illustrates in his litany of the those who have died and been laid to rest in Greenwood cemetery, including Red's uncle. Discussing the black inhabitants of the segregated graveyard, Canewell contends that they were never afforded a fair shake, either in life or death: "God don't give you no chances. The devil let you roll the dice. See if you crap out" (51). Floyd, nonetheless, resolutely will take his chances to pursue his dream, to make a name for himself as a musician, much in the way Levee does in *Ma Rainey's Black Bottom.*

Figuratively speaking, the import of the Madison Square Garden fight, which really took place in 1946, the fight between Joe Louis and Billy Conn, is much more than the black heavyweight champion defending his title. It embodies the struggle between the whites and blacks in this Pittsburgh community and the struggle for recognition and profit between the enterprising and talented black artist and the equally enterprising and exploitive white record producer. With each comment that sports announcer Don Dunphy makes, Wilson provides a visual portrait of a black man's struggle to be empowered as well, for it is Lewis who knocks Conn on his back; Conn the white fighter is under the "boot" of the black man, or, to paraphrase Hedley's words: "Because he know the place of the black man is not at the foot of a white man's boot . . ." (67). This fight foreshadows Hedley's prophetic advice to Floyd regarding the relationship between Floyd and the disreputable manager T. L. Hall, whose reputation is unknown to the starstruck musician: "You watch your back! The white man got a big plan against you. He look to knock you down" (71). Not heeding Hedley's advice, Floyd will be knocked down later by his manager. As a result, Floyd will no longer be able to trust his manager once he learns that T. L. Hall made Red Carter's cousin the victim of an insurance scam.

In this play and others the male characters fail to understand women, though they all do revere their mothers. Mothers, whether natural or surrogate, are portrayed by Wilson and perceived, for the most part, by male characters with much warmth and regard. This proves to be the case in *Ma Rainey's Black Bottom* with Levee and his mother; in *Fences* with Rose, her natural son Cory, and her stepson Lyons; in *The Piano Lesson* with Mama Ola and Boy Willie; and in *Seven Guitars* with Floyd and his mother and with Red Carter and his mother. Some characters serve as surrogate mothers too in Wilson's plays, such as the mother of the blues, Ma Rainey, in *Ma Rainey's Black Bottom;* the community griot Aunt Ester in *Two Trains Running;* and the local black healer Miss Sarah Divine in *Seven Guitars.*

In a *New York Times* article entitled "Living on Mother's Prayer" Wilson compares himself to the character Red Carter in dreading the day of his mother's passing, of having to wear a white carnation as he did on Mother's Day in 1983: "A world without the shelter and sustenance of a mother's prayer is, when you first encounter it, an alien place. . . . So much of who I am and the manner of man that I have become is because of who she is. . . . She knew and taught that we all have our hands in the soup, that we all make music play just so, that we can make of our lives what we will."[15] Accordingly, in *Seven Guitars* Wilson pays homage to mothers, even in the "Note from the Playwright" that prefaces the play. After Vera makes crepe paper carnations for Mother's Day, Red Carter selects a red carnation because his mother is still alive.

Wilson devotes much dialogue to the folklore of roosters in *Seven Guitars*. Floyd wishes he had a BB gun to shoot Miss Tillery's rooster, and Canewell speaks in great detail about the folk beliefs attributed to roosters. Canewell's description of roosters hailing from various regions of the country—Alabama, Georgia, and Mississippi—conveys as well a composite description of Floyd Barton's personality. The word *rooster,* a slang expression for *man,* was employed from the 1950s until the 1970s. Canewell says that the neighbor's rooster crows so frequently that it might be from Alabama, and that an Alabama rooster loves to hear its own voice. He elaborates that the bird's motives are unknown and that it is "no good for nobody" (60), similar to Louise's description of Floyd to Vera earlier in the play, "Floyd don't mean nobody no good" (31). Likewise, Canewell describes a Georgia rooster that he says thinks "it's a dog" (60), akin to Louise's description of Floyd to Vera when she ponders whether to go with him to Chicago "So he can dog you around some more up there" (31). Furthermore, Canewell's description of the Mississippi rooster, who crows both to let his presence be known and to warn "if somebody disturbs the hens in the barnyard," bears a metaphorical resemblance to Floyd (60).

First among these allusions is the description of Miss Tillery's rooster who crows every time Floyd's name is mentioned. Second, the others hear Floyd's recording, announcing his presence. Third, like a rooster in the barnyard proclaiming his dominant status among hens, Floyd physically reclaims Vera, who was dancing with Red after the Joe Louis fight. And, fourth, Vera questions the credibility of Canewell's characterization of roosters just as she questions the credibility of Louise's unflattering characterization of Floyd.

Canewell's tale that no one heard roosters crow until after the Emancipation Proclamation is even more telling. He contends that roosters did not crow during the time of slavery because there was nothing to celebrate. In the same vein Floyd, ready to make his mark as a blues artist, is literally severed from realizing his dream by a wound to his windpipe inflicted by Hedley later in act 2. Earlier in act 1 Hedley severs the throat of the rooster with his machete while uttering these prophetic words: "Your black ass be dead like the rooster now. You mark what Hedley say" (64). In act 2 Hedley makes Floyd the marked man. Hedley's mark, his emancipation, will be the stolen money he seizes from Floyd in their scuffle near the unearthed goldenseal plant which he thinks is the money from the imaginary Buddy Bolden. Moreover, when Hedley tells the others as he plays whist that "The rooster is the king of the barnyard. He like the black man. He king," Wilson foreshadows Hedley's victory and Floyd's final demise, for Hedley's first name is King (61).

The rooster is a significant metaphor in Wilson's play. Later in act 2 Red's comments about the rooster to Louise, Vera, and Ruby allude to the final confrontation between Hedley and Floyd,

## SEVEN GUITARS

directly to Hedley and his machete. In the past, Red says, a rooster was sufficient to protect a person's property, but now people need guns to protect themselves and their property from crazy individuals who threaten them with knives and meat cleavers. Also relevant is Red's tale about his bout with bad luck. Three years ago, Red accidentally broke a mirror, and he believes that he has four years of bad luck left with which to contend. This tale of bad luck is interrupted when he espies seven birds sitting on a fence nearby, posturing before a dog before scattering to the wind. Both the tale of Red's bad luck and the observation allude to the number seven—to the number of friends and to Floyd, who will be ill-fated and scattered to the wind when those angels escort him to heaven.

After listening to Red's story, Vera recalls that she was awakened by the sound the birds's wings in flight and the song they made. The fact that Floyd never returns to their bed that night and that the long night seems to transform into daylight instantly is Wilson's poetic rendering of Vera's epiphany, replete with a visual pun on her character's illumination. The sound of song and the image of flight relate to Floyd: the recording of "That's All Right," his flight from the police, and the escorted flight of his soul after his burial. The events that occur shortly thereafter lend further credence to this argument. A commotion is heard over the fence in Miss Tillery's yard: a dog is heard barking; a rooster crows; and the sound of a woman wailing is heard. Both the image of a dog and of a rooster are associated with Floyd. In Wilson's play the dog, the rooster, the birds in flight, and the song they make are signifiers, with Floyd being the subject of interpretation, the signified.

Yet in act 2, abiding by the linear constraints of plot line, the cacophony of sound heard arises from over the neighbor's fence, and the woman wailing is Miss Tillery. She is mourning the death of her twenty-seven-year-old son, Willard Ray "Poochie" Tillery, who was shot by a police officer while trying to flee from a robbery at the loan offices of Metro Finance, a robbery involving two other accomplices. One of the fleeing accomplices will later turn out to be Floyd Barton. Within this fusion of oral and visual cacophony the present and the past merge, and Wilson skillfully evokes the image of Floyd and soon after his slayer, Hedley.

Hedley's partial absolution lies in his relationship with the much younger Ruby, a woman motivated by her compassion for the old man. They communicate. In the beginning of act 2 the relationship between Hedley and Ruby unfolds. Ruby somehow manages to penetrate Hedley's hegemonic discourse with her own history, or herstory. While asking Hedley to make her a soft mattress from the discarded feathers of the chickens he slaughters, Ruby compares the innocence of the slaughtered rooster to her lover Leroy who was murdered. Elmore, a rival lover, murdered Leroy while he was in a barbershop. Elmore's overwhelming passion was suffocating the free-spirited Ruby, so she left him for Leroy. Ruby loved neither. This discussion of death leads to Buddy Bolden, and Ruby out of curiosity inquires who he is. Hedley replies that the musician was his namesake; his father, who was a trumpet player, thought that "Buddy Bolden was a god . . ." (67). Hedley takes pride in this name, even killing another black man who ridiculed it.

## *SEVEN GUITARS*

Hedley discloses that many assume he is crazy because he refuses to be subordinate to the white man. Like Jesus, Hedley claims, he is a prideful man, proud to be a son of his father. If Hedley could have a male child, maybe that child would be like Moses, a leader of his people, a leader like the legendary black nationalist Marcus Garvey. Names are of utmost importance to Hedley. When Hedley congratulates Red about the birth of his baby boy, he asks the child's name. Red responds that the child's name is "Mister," as in "Mr. Mister Carter," a name which Hedley believes will command respect (40). Red's son's name will be within the tradition of the names of prominent black men such as Marcus Garvey, famed leader of the Back to Africa movement; Toussaint l'Ouverture, liberator of Haiti; or prizefighter Joe Louis, after whom Hedley might name his child.

The audience comprehends how Hedley creates such a lasting impression upon Ruby. Ruby has suffered indignities. Like Hedley, Ruby's identity is of utmost importance. She refuses to be subordinate in any relationship, to suffer the insatiable sexual appetite of Elmore, to be objectified by another. Hedley too has maintained distance to preserve his identity and dreams in his platonic relationship with Louise. Consequently Ruby's personal decision to make Hedley believe that he is the father of her child, for either lover could be the baby's father, is her gift to the stoically proud Hedley, whom she admires. At least Ruby enables Hedley to have one facet of his dream fulfilled. Vera also will provide Floyd with one facet of his dream when she agrees to accompany Floyd to Chicago, but she will purchase a ticket to return to Pittsburgh if she changes her mind, considering Floyd's past infidelity. In Ruby's and Vera's relationships with men Wilson as a male playwright has stepped "around to the other side of the table" and captured in their behavior toward men from the woman's perspective.[16]

    *Seven Guitars* ends with the outcome of Hedley's violent act, echoed in the title of Floyd's song "That's All Right," which is heard on Vera's record player as the remaining friends discuss the ensuing police investigation. Hedley's culpability is a moot point. The question of guilt is not relevant. The importance of the chronological sequence of events which led to Floyd's demise appears inconsequential, and the audience is transported back, through song, to the beginning of Wilson's play. Wilson leads the audience back to the apparition of the six figures at the funeral who led their friend to the next world, as Vera recounts: "Them six men was holding him up. He come right out the casket just like they laid him in there and was floating up in the air. I could see where they was carrying him. They were all floating up in the sky . . ." (106).

    To conclude, akin to the Greeks concept of *moira,* or fate, the apparition of six figures represents the part each character plays in the course of Floyd's brief life, the part each assumes in the course of his or her own life, and their personal songs continue as narratives to be completed with some dreams yet to be fulfilled. Subsequently, as Louise, Vera, Red, and Ruby leave the stage, each awaiting destiny, only Canewell and Hedley remain onstage, functioning like a Euripidean chorus providing the befitting lyrical element so invested in Wilson's play. To Canewell's call, "I thought I heard Buddy Bolden say . . .," Hedley appropriately responds, "What he say?" and finally, "I thought I heard Buddy Bolden say . . ." (106). Then Hedley releases the crumpled bills from his grasp which fall like ashes upon the ground, and from those ashes arises Floyd, his spirit soaring like a Phoenix, symbolizing the impression he has made upon each character's life.

# Chapter One: Understanding August Wilson as an African American Playwright

1. Samuel G. Freedman, "A Voice from the Streets," *New York Times Magazine,* March 15, 1987, p. 49.

2. August Wilson, *Three Plays,* ed. Paul Carter Harrison (Pittsburgh: University of Pittsburgh Press, 1984), xi.

3. Freedman, "A Voice from the Streets," 49.

4. Henry Louis Gates Jr., "The Chitlin Circuit," *New Yorker* (February 3, 1997): 44.

5. The dates listed identify Broadway premieres. Prior to their Broadway debuts, several of Wilson's plays premiered at the Yale Repertory Theater in New Haven, Connecticut: *Ma Rainey's Black Bottom* on April 6, 1984; *Fences* on April 30, 1985; *Joe Turner's Come and Gone* on April 29, 1986; *The Piano Lesson* on November 26, 1987; and *Two Trains Running* on March 27, 1990. *Seven Guitars,* Wilson's most recent play, opened at the Goodman Theater in Chicago on January 21, 1995.

6. Robert Brustein, "The Lesson of *The Piano Lesson,*" *New Republic* (May 21, 1990): 28.

7. Robert Brustein, "Subsidized Separatism," *New Republic* (August 19 & 26, 1996): 40.

8. John Fleming, "A Casting Call," *St. Petersburg Times,* March 7, 1997, p. 2D.

9. Gates, "The Chitlin Circuit," 48. For further discussion of Wilson's controversial views regarding African American theater, see Douglas O. Barnett, "Up for the Challenge," in *Forum:* "Plowing August Wilson's Ground: Four Commentaries on the Cultural Diversity Debate," *American Theater* 13.10 (1996): 60; Alan Gerstle, "Not Radical Enough," in *Forum:* "Plowing August Wilson's Ground: Four Com-

mentaries on the Cultural Diversity Debate," *American Theater* 13.10 (1996): 59; Paul Goldberger, "From Page to Stage: Race and the Theater," *New York Times,* January 22, 1997, pp. C11ff; William Grimes, "Face-to-Face Encounter on Race in the Theater," *New York Times,* January 29, 1997, pp. C9–10; Jack Kroll, "And in This Corner . . . : A Black Playwright and White Critic Duke It Out," *Newsweek* (February 10, 1997): 65; James Leverett et al., "Beyond Black and White: 'On Cultural Power': 13 Commentaries," *American Theater* 14.5 (1997): 14ff; Richard Schechner, "In Praise of Promiscuity," in *Forum:* "Plowing August Wilson's Ground: Four Commentaries on the Cultural Diversity Debate," *American Theater* 13.10 (1996): 58–59; August Wilson, "I Want a Black Director," in *May All Your Fences Have Gates: Essays on the Drama of August Wilson,* ed. Alan Nadel (Iowa City: University of Iowa Press, 1994), 200–204; Marion X, "Out on a Limb, Reaching Back," in *Forum:* "Plowing August Wilson's Ground: Four Commentaries on the Cultural Diversity Debate," *American Theater* 13.10 (1996): 60; and Margo Jefferson et al., "Beyond the Wilson-Brustein Debate," *Theater* 27.2 & 3 (1997): 9–41.

10. Freedman, "A Voice from the Streets," 40.

11. Michael Awkward, "'The Crookeds with the Straights': Fences, Race, and the Politics of Adaptation," in *May All Your Fences Have Gates: Essays on the Drama of August Wilson,* ed. Alan Nadel (Iowa City: University of Iowa Press, 1994), 208.

12. Harry J. Elam Jr., "Of Angels and Transcendence: An Analysis of *Fences* by August Wilson and *Roosters* by Milcha Sanchez-Scott," in *Staging Difference: Cultural Pluralism in American Theatre and Drama,* ed. Marc Maufort (New York: Peter Lang, 1995), 299.

13. Charles R. Lyons, "Shepard's Family Trilogy and the Conventions of Modern Realism," in *Rereading Shepard,* ed. Leonard Chaise (New York: St. Martin's Press, 1993), 115–30.

14. Dennis Watlington, "Hurdling Fences," *Vanity Fair* 356 (1989): 106.

15. William Plummer, "Street Talk: Hearing Voices Makes Playwright August Wilson the Talent He Is," March 24, 1997. [Online] Available from http://pathfinder.com/people/960513/features/wilson.html.

16. Sandra G. Shannon, *The Dramatic Vision of August Wilson* (Washington, D.C.: Howard University Press, 1995), 234. This work also contains critical and theatrical reviews and extensive biographical details of Wilson's life.

## Chapter Two: *Ma Rainey's Black Bottom*

1. August Wilson, *Ma Rainey's Black Bottom* (New York: Plume, 1981), xv. Subsequent references to this edition are noted parenthetically.

2. Francis Davis, *The History of the Blues: The Roots, The Music, The People from Charley Patton to Robert Cray* (New York: Hyperion, 1995), 47–48.

3. Bill Moyers, "August Wilson's America: A Conversation with Bill Moyers," *American Theater* 7.6 (1989): 14.

4. Davis, *The History of the Blues,* 243.

5. Ibid., 74.

6. Kim Pereira, *August Wilson and the African-American Odyssey* (Urbana: University of Illinois Press, 1995), 15.

7. Imamu Amiri Baraka [as LeRoi Jones], *Blues People: The Negro Experience in White America and the Music that Developed from It* (New York: Morrow Quill, 1963), x.

8. Craig Werner, "August Wilson's Burden: The Function of Neoclassical Jazz," in *May All Your Fences Have Gates: Essays on the*

*Drama of August Wilson,* ed. Alan Nadel (Iowa City: University of Iowa Press, 1994), 40.

9. John Timpane, "Filling the Time: Reading History in the Drama of August Wilson," in *May All Your Fences Have Gates: Essays on the Drama of August Wilson,* ed. Alan Nadel (Iowa City: University of Iowa Press, 1994), 75.

10. James C McKelly, "Hymns of Sedition: Portraits of the Artist in Contemporary African-American Drama," *Arizona Quarterly: A Journal of American Literature, Culture, and Theory* 48.1 (1992): 99.

## Chapter Three: *Fences*

1. August Wilson, *Fences* (New York: Plume, 1986), 61. Subsequent references to this edition are noted parenthetically.

2. Freedman, "A Voice from the Streets," 40.

3. Awkward, "'The Crookeds with the Straights,'" 216.

4. Lyons, "Shepard's Family Trilogy and the Conventions of Modern Realism," 129.

5. Elam, "Of Angels and Transcendence," 297.

## Chapter Four: *Joe Turner's Come and Gone*

1. Wilson, *Three Plays,* xiv.

2. Kim Powers, "An Interview with August Wilson," *Theater* 16.1 (1984): 53.

3. Shannon, *The Dramatic Vision of August Wilson,* 126.

4. Langston Hughes, *Selected Poems* (New York: Alfred A. Knopf, 1959), 3.

5. Jack Kroll, "August Wilson's Come to Stay," *Newsweek* (April 11, 1988): 82.

6. Beverly J. Robinson, "Africanisms and the Study of Folklore," in *Africanisms in American Culture,* ed. Joseph E. Holloway (Bloomington: Indiana University Press, 1990), 215. For a more extensive discussion of the juba and its relationship to Wilson's play, see Mary L. Bogumil, "'Tomorrow Never Comes': Songs of Cultural Identity in August Wilson's *Joe Turner's Come and Gone," Theatre Journal* 46.4 (1994): 463–76.

7. Robinson, "Africanisms and the Study of Folklore," 215.

8. August Wilson, *Joe Turner's Come and Gone* (New York: Plume, 1988), 55. Subsequent references to this edition are noted parenthetically.

9. Richard Pettengill, "The Historical Perspective: An Interview with August Wilson," in *August Wilson: A Casebook,* ed. Marilyn Elkins (New York: Garland, 1994), 223.

10. Ronald Takaki, *A Different Mirror: A History of Multicultural America* (Boston: Little, Brown, 1993), 344.

11. Ibid.

12. Wilson, *Three Plays,* xiii.

13. William W. Cook, "Change the Joke and Slip the Yoke: Traditions of Afro-American Satire," *Journal of Ethnicity* 13.1 (1985): 112.

14. Ibid., 120.

15. Baraka, *Blues People,* 51.

16. Houston A. Baker Jr., *Blues, Ideology, and Afro-American Literature: A Vernacular Theory* (Chicago: University of Chicago Press, 1984), 4.

17. Shannon, *The Dramatic Vision of August Wilson,* 137.

18. Sandra G. Shannon, "The Good Christian's Come and Gone: The Shifting Role of Christianity in August Wilson Plays," *MELUS* 16.3 (1989): 127.

19. Baker, *Blues, Ideology, and Afro-American Literature,* 5.

20. Wilson, *Three Plays,* xiv.

21. Linda Metzger et al., eds., *Black Writers: A Selection of Sketches from Contemporary Authors* (Detroit: Gale, 1989), 605.

22. Ibid.

## Chapter Five: *The Piano Lesson*

1. August Wilson, *The Piano Lesson* (New York: Plume, 1990), 1. Subsequent references to this edition are noted parenthetically.

2. Alan Nadel, ed., *May All Your Fences Have Gates: Essays on the Drama of August Wilson* (Iowa City: University of Iowa Press, 1994), 3.

3. Pereira, *August Wilson and the African-American Odyssey,* 86.

4. Kim Marra, "Ma Rainey and the Boyz: Gender Ideology in August Wilson's Broadway Canon," in *August Wilson: A Casebook,* ed. Marilyn Elkins (New York: Garland, 1994), 144–45.

5. August Wilson, "How to Write a Play Like August Wilson," *New York Times,* March 10, 1991, p. 17.

6. Anne Fleche, "The History Lesson: Authenticity and Anachronism in August Wilson's Plays," in *May All Your Fences Have Gates: Essays on the Drama of August Wilson,* ed. Alan Nadel (Iowa City: University of Iowa Press, 1994), 10.

7. Michael Morales, "Ghosts on the Piano: August Wilson and the Representation of Black American History," in *May All Your Fences Have Gates: Essays on the Drama of August Wilson,* ed. Alan Nadel (Iowa City: University of Iowa Press, 1994), 111.

## Chapter Six: *Two Trains Running*

1. Daniel M. Johnson and Rex R. Campbell, *Black Migration in America: A Social Demographic History* (Durham, N.C.: Duke University Press, 1981), 154.

2. Ibid., 152.

3. James H. Cone, *Martin & Malcolm & America* (Maryknoll, N.Y.: Orbis Books, 1991), 90.

4. August Wilson, *Two Trains Running* (New York: Plume, 1992), 9. Subsequent references to this edition are noted parenthetically.

5. See Clarence Major, ed. and intro., *From Juba to Jive: A Dictionary of African-American Slang* (New York: Penguin, 1994), 220.

6. Mark William Rocha, "American History as 'Loud Talking' in *Two Trains Running,*" in *May All Your Fences Have Gates: Essays on the Drama of August Wilson,* ed. Alan Nadel (Iowa City: University of Iowa Press, 1994), 116.

7. Ibid.

8. Ibid., 118.

9. Henry Louis Gates Jr., *The Signifying Monkey: A Theory of Afro-American Literary Criticism* (New York: Oxford University Press, 1988), 42.

10. Shannon, *The Dramatic Vision of August Wilson,* 174. For a further discussion of the African griot and its role in African culture, see Thomas A. Hale, *Scribe, Griot, and Novelist: Narrative Interpreters of the Songhay Empire* (Gainesville: University of Florida Press, 1990), 30–46.

11. August Wilson, "How to Write a Play Like August Wilson," *New York Times,* March 10, 1991, p. 5.

12. Daniel R. Fusfeld and Timothy Bates, *The Political Economy of the Urban Ghetto* (Carbondale: Southern Illinois University Press, 1984), 213.

13. Booker T. Washington, *Up from Slavery* (New York: Dover, 1995), 107.

14. Sandra G. Shannon, "The Ground on Which I Stand: August Wilson's Perspective on African American Women," in *May All Your Fences Have Gates: Essays on the Drama of August Wilson,* ed. Alan Nadel (Iowa City: University of Iowa Press, 1994), 162.

15. Pettengill, "The Historical Perspective," 208.

16. Richard Pettengill, "Alternatives . . . Opposites . . . Convergences: "An Interview with Lloyd Richards," in *August Wilson: A Casebook,* ed. Marilyn Elkins (New York: Garland, 1994), 202–3.

17. Cone, *Martin & Malcolm & America,* 317.

18. Rocha, "American History as 'Loud Talking' in *Two Trains Running,*" 119.

## Chapter Seven: *Seven Guitars*

1. August Wilson, *Seven Guitars* (New York: Dutton, 1996), 8. Subsequent references to this edition are noted parenthetically.

2. John Lahr, "Black and Blues: *Seven Guitars,* a New Chapter in August Wilson's Ten-Play Cycle," *New Yorker* (April 15, 1996): 100.

3. Ibid.

4. Shannon, "The Ground on Which I Stand," 151.

5. Ibid., 162.

6. Ibid.

7. Harry J. Elam Jr., "August Wilson's Women," in *May All Your Fences Have Gates: Essays on the Drama of August Wilson,* ed. Alan Nadel (Iowa City: University of Iowa Press, 1994), 165.

8. Ibid., 178.

9. Harnett T. Kane, quoted in Donald M. Marquis, *In Search of Buddy Bolden: First Man of Jazz* (Baton Rouge: Louisiana State University Press, 1978), 94.

10. For a discussion of Bolden and references to him as the "King," see Marquis, *In Search of Buddy Bolden,* 4, 9.

11. bell hooks, *Yearning: Race, Gender, and Cultural Politics* (Boston: South End Press, 1990), 18.

12. Jeff Yang, "Nomenculture," *Village Voice,* January 4, 1994, p. 18.

13. Apart from the title, the play contains in its context many biblical references—including Hedley's brand of religiosity throughout the play, and especially when he talks about fathering a messiah to Ruby in act 2 and Floyd's singing of "The Lord's Prayer" in act 1. The number seven resonates with references to both the Old and New Testaments. This number generally implies the presence or lack of integrity in life. For example in the Old Testament, Cain is avenged seven times, Lamech seven times seventy (Gen. 4:15); there are seven fat years and seven lean years in Egypt (Gen. 4:24); Samson's hair is bound in seven locks (Judg. 16:13); Ruth is considered better than seven sons (Ruth 4:15); the Israelites march seven times around Jericho (Josh. 6:1); the days of creation are followed by the seventh day of rest (Gen. 2:1–3); and the number seven is frequently used in rituals, such as rites of purification (Lev. 12–15). Likewise, in the New Testament, Jesus multiplies seven loaves into seven baskets of fragments (Matt. 15:34–37; Mark 8:5–8); the evil spirit who returns after exorcism brings forth seven other spirits (Matt. 12:45; Luke 11:26); there are seven demons cast out of Mary Magdalene (Luke 8:2); in the Book of Revelation there are seven churches, seven lamps, seven stars, seven spirits, seven seals, seven trumpets, and so on; and in Luke the number of times a person should be forgiven is seven (17:4), while in Matthew the amount increases to seven times seventy— meaning an unlimited amount of times and forgiveness leads to a new type of integrity or fullness in life (18:22, 35).

14. Lahr, "Black and Blues," 100.

15. August Wilson, "Living on Mother's Prayer," *New York Times,* May 12, 1996, IV: 13.

16. Shannon, "The Ground on Which I Stand," 151.

# BIBLIOGRAPHY

## Published Works by August Wilson

### Plays

*Ma Rainey's Black Bottom.* New York: Plume/Penguin, 1981; [acting edition] New York: Samuel French, 1984.

*The Janitor.* In *Short Pieces from the New Dramatists.* Ed. Stan Chervin. New York: Broadway Play Publishing, 1985.

*Fences.* New York: Plume/Penguin, 1986; [acting edition] New York: Samuel French, 1987.

*Fences/Ma Rainey's Black Bottom.* Harmondsworth, U.K.: Penguin, 1988.

*Joe Turner's Come and Gone.* New York: Plume/Penguin, 1988; [acting edition] New York: Samuel French, 1988.

*The Piano Lesson.* New York: Plume/Penguin, 1990.

*August Wilson: Three Plays.* Ed. Paul Carter Harrison. Pittsburgh: University of Pittsburgh Press, 1991.

*Two Trains Running.* New York: Plume/Penguin, 1992.

*Seven Guitars.* New York: Dutton, 1996; [acting edition] New York: Samuel French, 1996.

### Poems

"Bessie." *Black Lines* 1 (Summer 1971): 68.

"Morning Song." *Black Lines* 1 (Summer 1971): 68.

"For Malcolm X and Others." *Negro Digest* 18 (September 1971): 58.

"Muhammad Ali." *Black World* 1 (September 1972): 60–61.

"Theme One: The Variations." In *The Poetry of Black America: Anthology of the Twentieth Century,* edited by Arnold Adoff. New York: Harper and Row, 1973.

# BIBLIOGRAPHY

## *Selected Articles*

"Preface." In *August Wilson: Three Plays,* edited by Paul Carter Harrison. Pittsburgh: University of Pittsburgh Press, 1991, vii-xiv.

"How to Write a Play Like August Wilson." *New York Times,* March 10, 1991, pp. 5, 17. Wilson explains his influences and discusses his plays.

"The Legacy of Malcolm X." *Life* 15 (December 1992): 84–94. Echoes of black nationalism in Wilson's work.

"I Want a Black Director." In *May All Your Fences Have Gates: Essays on the Drama of August Wilson,* edited by Alan Nadel, 200–204. Iowa City: University of Iowa Press, 1994. Wilson explains why only a black director can understand the specific cultural implications of *Fences.*

"The Ground on Which I Stand." *American Theater* 13.7 (1996): 14–16, 71–74. Wilson's controversial speech about the paucity of opportunities for black directors, playwrights, and actors within the white-controlled theater.

"Living on Mother's Prayer." *New York Times,* May 12, 1996, IV: 13. Wilson discusses his relationship with his mother and its impact on *Seven Guitars.*

## *Interviews*

DiGaetani, John L. "August Wilson." In *A Search for a Postmodern Theater: Interviews with Contemporary Playwrights,* edited by John L. DiGaetani, 275–84. Westport, Conn.: Greenwood Press, 1991. Wilson elaborates upon the significance of music, particularly the blues, in his plays.

Moyers, Bill. "August Wilson's American: A Conversation with Bill Moyers." *American Theater* 7.6 (1989): 13–17, 54. Wilson explains why his plays are always set in the past and why the blues play a significant role in his plays.

BIBLIOGRAPHY

Pettengill, Richard. "The Historical Perspective: An Interview with August Wilson." In *August Wilson: A Casebook,* edited by Marilyn Elkins, 207–26. New York: Garland, 1994. Wilson addresses in-depth the craft of playwriting from *Ma Rainey's Black Bottom* to *Seven Guitars.*

Powers, Kim. "An Interview with August Wilson." *Theater* 16.1 (1984): 50–55. Wilson discusses his growth as a playwright and major influences on him.

Schafer, Yvonne. "An Interview with August Wilson." *Journal of Dramatic Theory and Criticism* 4 (1989): 161–73. Wilson discusses his approach to writing plays within a distinctly African American cultural context.

Shannon, Sandra G. "Blues, History, and Dramaturgy: An Interview with August Wilson." *African American Review* 27.4 (1993): 539–59. Wilson discusses the cultural and political agendas underlying his plays.

Watlington, Dennis. "Hurdling Fences." *Vanity Fair* 356 (April 1989): 102–13. Wilson addresses his role as a black writer in American theater.

## Selected Works on August Wilson

### *Collections of Essays*

Elkins, Marilyn. *August Wilson: A Casebook.* New York: Garland, 1994. A collection of essays on Wilson's plays and interviews with Wilson and Lloyd Richards.

Nadel, Alan, ed. *May All Your Fences Have Gates: Essays on the Drama of August Wilson.* Iowa City: University of Iowa Press, 1994. A collection of sophisticated critical articles on Wilson's plays, including an annotated bibliography of Wilson's play reviews.

# BIBLIOGRAPHY

## *Books*

Pereira, Kim. *August Wilson and the African-American Odyssey.* Urbana: University of Illinois Press, 1995. An extensive analysis of the themes—separation, migration, and spiritual reunion—and the significance of African folklore in *Ma Rainey's Black Bottom, Fences, Joe Turner's Come and Gone,* and *The Piano Lesson.*

Shannon, Sandra G. *The Dramatic Vision of August Wilson.* Washington, D.C.: Howard University Press, 1995. A detailed overview of Wilson's plays through *Two Trains Running,* particularly useful for biographical information on the playwright; includes Wilson's, lead actors', directors', and critics' discussions of the plays.

## *Critical Essays and Selected Reviews*

Arthur, Thomas H. "Looking for My Relatives: The Political Implications of 'Family' in Selected Work of Athol Fugard and August Wilson." *South African Theatre Journal* 6.2 (1992): 5–16.

Barnett, Douglas O. "Up for the Challenge." *Forum:* "Plowing August Wilson's Ground: Four Commentaries on the Cultural Diversity Debate." *American Theater* 13.10 (1996): 60. An interpretation and response to Wilson's "The Ground on Which I Stand."

Birdwell, Christine. "Death as a Fastball on the Outside Corner: *Fences'* Troy Maxson and the American Dream." *Aethlon: The Journal of Sport Literature* 8.1 (1990): 87–96. Baseball as a complex metaphor in Wilson's play.

Bogumil, Mary L. "'Tomorrow Never Comes': Songs of Cultural Identity in August Wilson's *Joe Turner's Come and Gone." Theatre Journal* 46.4 (1994): 463–76. An examination of the juba and its cultural relevance to Wilson's play.

Brustein, Robert. "The Lesson of *The Piano Lesson." New Republic,*

May 21, 1990, pp. 28–30. An unflattering assessment of *The Piano Lesson* and a discussion of Wilson's dramatic themes and artistic goals.

————. "Subsidized Separatism." *New Republic,* August 19 & 26, 1996, pp. 39–42. A critical response to Wilson's "The Ground on Which I Stand."

Ching, Mei-Ling. "Wrestling against History." *Theater* 19.3 (1988): 70–71. Discussion of Christian and African elements in *The Piano Lesson.*

Elam, Harry J., Jr. "Of Angels and Transcendence: An Analysis of *Fences* by August Wilson and *Roosters* by Milcha Sanchez-Scott." In *Staging Difference: Cultural Pluralism in American Theatre and Drama,* edited by Marc Maufort, 287–300. New York: Peter Lang, 1995. Addresses the significance of a retrospective structure.

Fleming. John. "A Casting Call." *St. Petersburg Times,* March 7, 1997, pp. D1–2. Includes an interview with Lloyd Richards.

Freedman, Samuel G. "A Voice from the Streets." *New York Times Magazine,* March 15, 1987, pp. 36, 40, 49, 70. An overview of Wilson's life, works, and influences.

Gates, Henry Louis, Jr. "The Chitlin Circuit." *New Yorker* (February 3, 1997): 44–55. A scholarly response to Wilson's "The Ground on Which I Stand."

Gerstle, Alan. "Not Radical Enough." *Forum:* "Plowing August Wilson's Ground: Four Commentaries on the Cultural Diversity Debate." *American Theater* 13.10 (1996): 59. A sociological response to Wilson's "The Ground on Which I Stand."

Glover, Margaret E. "Two Notes on August Wilson: The Songs of a Marked Man." *Theater* 19.3 (1988): 69–70. Explores how many of Wilson's characters are affected directly and indirectly by the blues music they sing and play.

## BIBLIOGRAPHY

Goldberger, Paul. "From Page to Stage: Race and the Theater." *New York Times,* January 22, 1997, pp. C11, 14. Commentary on Wilson's "The Ground on Which I Stand."

Grimes, William. "Face-to-Face Encounter on Race in the Theater." *New York Times,* January 29, 1997, pp. C9–10. A political interpretation of Wilson's "The Ground on Which I Stand."

Kroll, Jack. "And in This Corner . . . : A Black Playwright and White Critic Duke It Out." *Newsweek* (February 10, 1997): 65. Addresses Robert Brustein's critical response to Wilson's "The Ground on Which I Stand."

———. "August Wilson's Come to Stay." *Newsweek* (April 11, 1988): 82. A positive assessment of *Joe Turner's Come and Gone* and an overview of Wilson's early plays.

Lahr, John. "Black and Blues: *Seven Guitars,* a New Chapter in August Wilson's Ten-Play Cycle." *New Yorker* (April 15, 1996): 99–101. Review of *Seven Guitars.*

Leverett, James, et al. "Beyond Black and White: 'On Cultural Power': 13 Commentaries." *American Theater* 14.5 (1997): 14–15, 53–56, 58–59. Artists and thinkers respond to issues addressed during the Wilson-Brustein debate.

McKelly, James C. "Hymns of Sedition: Portraits of the Artist in Contemporary African-American Drama." *Arizona Quarterly: A Journal of American Literature, Culture, and Theory* 48.1 (1992): 87–107. A socio-economic explanation of the inequitable relationship between black artists and the white recording industry.

Mills, Alice. "The Walking Blues: An Anthropological Approach to the Theater of August Wilson." *Black Scholar* 25.2 (1995): 30–35. An analysis of sacred African traditions and rituals as key components in Wilson's plays.

O'Neill, Michael. "August Wilson." In *American Playwrights Since*

# BIBLIOGRAPHY

*1945: A Guide to Scholarship, Criticism, and Performance,* edited by Philip C. Kolin, 518–27. Westport, Conn.: Greenwood Press, 1989. Bibliography and criticism of Wilson's plays.

Plum, Jay. "Blues, History, and the Dramaturgy of August Wilson." *African American Review* 27.4 (1993): 561–67. Applies Houston Baker's blues theory to Wilson's plays.

Rocha, Mark William. "Black Madness in August Wilson's 'Down the Line' Cycle." In *Madness in Drama,* edited by James Redmond, 191–201. Cambridge: Cambridge University Press, 1993.

Saunders, James Robert. "Essential Ambiguities in the Plays of August Wilson." *Hollins Critic* 32.5 (1995): 2–11. Saunders analyzes how the characters in Wilson's plays, up to *Two Trains Running,* retrieve their sense of history through the stories they tell. Particularly interesting is the discussion of Troy in *Fences,* a character who was denied an athletic career in integrated baseball like the Negro League's great players James "Cool Papa" Bell, Walter "Buck" Leonard, and Josh Gibson.

Schechner, Richard. "In Praise of Promiscuity." *Forum:* "Plowing August Wilson's Ground: Four Commentaries on the Cultural Diversity Debate." *American Theater* 13.10 (1996): 58–59. Varied interpretations of Wilson's "The Ground on Which I Stand."

Shafer, Yvonne. "August Wilson: A New Approach to Black Drama." *Zeitschrift fur Anglistik und Amerikanistik: A Quarterly of Language, Literature and Culture* 39.1 (1991): 17–27.

———. "Breaking Barriers: August Wilson." In *Staging Difference: Cultural Pluralism in American Theatre and Drama,* edited by Marc Maufort, 267–85. New York: Peter Lang, 1995. Critical interpretation of Wilson's plays and overview of theatrical reviews.

Shannon, Sandra G. "Conversing with the Past: *Joe Turner's Come and Gone* and *The Piano Lesson.*" *CEA Magazine: A Journal of the College English Association* 4.1 (1991): 33–42. Suggests that con-

# BIBLIOGRAPHY

temporary African American audience uses drama as a means of connecting with ancient past.

———. "From Lorraine Hansberry to August Wilson: An Interview with Lloyd Richards." *Callaloo* 14.1 (1991): 124–35. Richards speaks about his career in the theater and his relationship to Wilson.

———. "The Good Christian's Come and Gone: The Shifting Role of Christianity in August Wilson Plays." *MELUS* 16.3 (1989): 127–42. Explains the role of black men as blasphemers in Wilson's plays because God refuses to hear their prayers.

Smith, Philip E., II. "*Ma Rainey's Black Bottom:* Playing the Blues as Equipment for Living." In *Within the Dramatic Spectrum,* edited by V. Hartigan Karelisa, 177–86. Lanham, Md.: University of America Press, 1986.

Staples, Brent. "August Wilson." *Essence* 18 (August 1987): 51, 111, 113. Examines the oral tradition and blues music in Wilson's plays.

Wilde, Lisa. "Reclaiming the Past: Narrative and Memory in August Wilson's Two Trains Running." *Theater* 22.1 (1990): 73–74. An examination of the narrative construction in Wilson's play and his use of personal memory in creating characters

X, Marion. "Out on a Limb, Reaching Back." *Forum:* "Plowing August Wilson's Ground: Four Commentaries on the Cultural Diversity Debate." *American Theater* 13.10 (1996): 60. An interpretation of Wilson's "The Ground on Which I Stand."

# INDEX

## INDEX

INDEX